Facts You Didn't Know You Needed

Facts You Didn't Know You Needed...

Facts You Didn't Know You Needed...

*This book is inspired by and dedicated to
one of the most intelligent men I have met,
a true real life Indiana Jones of knowledge and travel.
SV... you know who you are. x*

Facts You Didn't Know You Needed...

CONTENTS

Facts You Didn't Know You Needed...

NOTE: or as I had originally intended to call it...

Learning on the Loo

Introduction

So, you've picked up this book. Congratulations! You've just taken the first step on a journey into the wonderfully weird, the astonishingly absurd, and the delightfully unexpected. This isn't your average collection of facts; it's a curated carnival of curiosities, a kaleidoscope of knowledge, and a veritable smorgasbord of strange but true statements. Prepare to be amazed, amused, and possibly slightly bewildered. We'll delve into the depths of the ocean, the vastness of space, and the intricate workings of the human mind. As the above note suggests this is an excellent way of entertaining yourself whilst you poop. No WiFi... no problem. For those of you who do not remember a world without the internet here is the solution to the modern problem of having no signal on your device...

The Surprising Sex Lives of Penguins

FORGET fluffy bunnies and playful kittens; the penguin world is where the real drama unfolds. These seemingly adorable flightless birds engage in mating rituals that would make even the most seasoned soap opera writer blush. Let's dive into the surprisingly complex – and sometimes downright bizarre – sex lives of penguins.

First, let's address the elephant (or perhaps, the emperor penguin) in the room: monogamy. While not universally practiced across all penguin species, many, like the iconic emperor penguins, form strong pair bonds, often lasting for multiple breeding seasons. But "monogamous" doesn't mean "exclusively loyal." Think of it more like a committed partnership with some... flexibility. Infidelity isn't unheard of, especially when resources are scarce or partners fail to return from fishing expeditions. It's a harsh, unforgiving world out there on the Antarctic ice, and survival – both of the individual and the offspring – is paramount.

The courtship rituals themselves are nothing short of spectacular. Imagine a rocky beach transformed into a bustling dance floor, with tuxedo-clad gentlemen (and ladies!) vying for attention. Emperor penguins, for example, engage in elaborate vocalizations, often described as "braying" or "trumpeting," to attract potential mates. These aren't gentle murmurs; these are powerful, resonant calls that carry across the icy landscape, announcing the presence of a potential partner.

But the vocalizations are just the beginning. Many penguin species incorporate impressive physical displays. Think synchronized swimming, but with a lot less chlorine and a lot more penguin charm. They may perform elaborate bowing, head-bobbing, and even pebble-presenting ceremonies. Yes, you read that correctly. Some penguin species, particularly the gentoo and chinstrap penguins, engage in a rather unique form of gift-giving. The males will meticulously collect pebbles, carefully constructing a nest. The quality and quantity of the pebble collection directly reflect the male's dedication and desirability – a real-life avian version of showing off your prized possessions. It's a testament to the intricate courtship rituals that these seemingly simple birds have developed.

The competition can be fierce. Picture a crowded beach, filled with hundreds of penguins all vying for a mate. Brawls and jostling are not uncommon, with males engaging in aggressive displays to assert dominance and secure a prime nesting spot. Size and strength do play a role, but cleverness and persistence are also valuable assets. This competitive environment ensures that only the fittest and most resourceful penguins will successfully reproduce, ensuring the survival of the species.

Once a pair has successfully bonded, the work doesn't end. Building a nest, incubating eggs, and raising chicks are collaborative efforts demanding significant energy and commitment. In emperor penguins, the dedication is particularly extreme. The female lays a single egg, then leaves the male to incubate it while she embarks on a perilous journey to the sea in search of food. The male will patiently stand guard over the egg for weeks, enduring harsh weather conditions and sometimes going without food himself. His survival hinges on his perseverance, a stark reminder of the commitment involved in penguin parenthood.

The breeding season is a time of high-stakes drama. Environmental factors, like the availability of food and the severity of the weather, can significantly impact reproductive success. A harsh winter or a shortage of fish can lead to increased mortality rates among both adults and chicks. This constant struggle for survival shapes the behaviours and strategies employed by penguins, reinforcing the importance of effective mating rituals and committed parental care.

The diversity of penguin species translates into a fascinating array of mating rituals. Different species utilize different strategies to attract mates and raise their young. For instance, some species have elaborate courtship dances that involve coordinated movements and vocalizations, while others rely on simple displays of dominance. The king penguin's courtship involves a more subdued approach, with less emphasis on vigorous displays and more on mutual recognition and cooperation.

The social structure of penguin colonies also plays a significant role in their mating behaviour. The dense populations and the competition for resources mean that penguins must carefully navigate social hierarchies to secure a mate and a breeding spot. These complex social dynamics are reflected in the timing of breeding, the location of nests, and even the aggression levels displayed during courtship. The social aspect of penguin life is as interesting as the mating rituals themselves. Observing a penguin colony is like watching a bustling, feathered metropolis with its own intricate social rules and hierarchies.

Beyond the romantic elements, the lives of penguins are shaped by the constant need to survive and adapt. Climate change, pollution, and human encroachment are significant threats to penguin populations worldwide. The success of their breeding cycles relies heavily on environmental factors. Sea ice levels, the abundance of prey fish, and the presence of predators all play critical roles in the survival of penguin chicks and adults. Studying their mating rituals allows scientists to gain valuable insights into the health and resilience of these fascinating creatures.

But the surprising sex lives of penguins are more than just a quirky anecdote. These unique behaviours provide valuable insights into evolutionary biology, animal behaviour, and social dynamics. They reveal the intricate adaptations that have allowed penguins to thrive in some of the most extreme environments on Earth. Their stories highlight the incredible resilience of these creatures, the power of committed partnerships, and the importance of adapting to a changing world. So next time you see a picture of an adorable penguin, remember the fascinating story of survival, competition, and surprising romance that plays out every breeding season. It's a story worth knowing, a testament to the unexpected depths within the seemingly simple lives of these extraordinary birds. The complexities of their behaviour serve as a constant reminder of nature's ingenuity and the fascinating variety of life on our planet. We've only just scratched the surface of understanding the full extent of penguin behaviour, and much more remains to be discovered.

Further research into penguin mating rituals will undoubtedly unearth even more surprising and fascinating details about these remarkable creatures. This area of study holds the potential to provide valuable insights not only into animal behaviour but also into the broader themes of social dynamics, adaptation, and survival strategies in harsh environments. The continued observation and study of penguin populations are crucial for understanding their ecological roles and for implementing effective conservation strategies to ensure their survival for generations to come. So, the next time you think about penguins, remember: it's not all just waddle and wobble. It's a world of complex social structures, competitive courtship, and a surprisingly intense romantic drama playing out on the icy stages of Antarctica and beyond. And that, my friends, is a fact worth knowing.

Natures Tiny Architects

FROM the seemingly simple elegance of a honeycomb to the labyrinthine complexity of an ant colony, the insect world reveals a breathtaking array of architectural marvels. These tiny creatures, often overlooked in our daily lives, possess an innate engineering prowess that rivals, and in some cases surpasses, human ingenuity. Their constructions aren't mere shelters; they are sophisticated, self-regulating systems, finely tuned to optimize resource use, defence, and social interaction. Let's delve into the miniature masterpieces crafted by nature's tiniest architects.

The honeybee's hexagonal honeycomb, a testament to mathematical precision, is perhaps the most iconic example of insect architecture. Each cell, perfectly formed and flawlessly consistent, maximizes storage space while minimizing the amount of wax used in construction. This isn't a random process; bees instinctively follow a blueprint dictated by their genetic programming, resulting in a structure of astonishing efficiency. The hexagonal shape, mathematically proven to be the most space-efficient polygon, allows for the seamless packing of countless cells, creating a remarkably strong and stable structure capable of supporting the weight of honey and the bustling activity of the hive. But the efficiency extends beyond mere geometry. The honeycomb's orientation is also meticulously calculated to optimize temperature regulation, with the cells angled to maximize sunlight exposure for warmth and minimize direct exposure during scorching periods. Studies have even shown that the bees subtly adjust the angle of the honeycomb depending on the time of year and the prevailing weather conditions. It's a truly dynamic structure, constantly adapting to its environment. Beyond the obvious structural brilliance, the honeycombs themselves are also incredibly hygienic, their slightly angled surfaces promoting drainage and preventing the accumulation of moisture or debris, minimizing the risk of bacterial or fungal contamination.

Moving beyond the honeybee's remarkable achievement, we encounter the subterranean cities of ants and termites, equally impressive feats of engineering. Ant colonies, often sprawling underground networks, can extend for many meters, comprising a vast system of interconnected tunnels, chambers, and galleries. These aren't haphazard burrowings; they are precisely engineered to accommodate the colony's diverse needs. Different areas are designated for specific purposes – nurseries for the larvae, storage chambers for food, and specialized chambers for the queen ant and her attendants. The ventilation system is also surprisingly sophisticated, with tunnels designed to ensure proper air circulation and temperature regulation within the colony. Some ant species even cultivate fungi within their nests, creating elaborate underground farms where they grow their food source. The complexity of these subterranean networks is staggering, often showcasing a remarkable level of division of labour and communication among the colony's inhabitants. Each ant seemingly knows its role and its place within the larger societal structure. These intricate networks are not just living spaces; they are dynamic ecosystems supporting thousands, or even millions, of individual ants. Their construction is a continuous process of expansion and adaptation, responding to the colony's growth and changing needs.

Termite mounds, found in tropical and subtropical regions, are even more awe-inspiring examples of insect architecture. These towering structures, often reaching several meters in height, are not simply piles of dirt; they are complex, self-regulating ecosystems optimized for temperature and humidity control. The mounds are typically composed of intricate networks of tunnels and chambers, with strategically placed vents and chimneys that regulate air flow and maintain a stable internal environment. This is crucial for the survival of the colony, as termites are highly susceptible to fluctuations in temperature and humidity. The design of these structures is particularly impressive given the lack of centralized control; each termite contributes to the construction process based on simple, instinctive behaviours, yet the overall result is a highly functional and remarkably sophisticated structure. Some termite mounds even incorporate sophisticated sun-tracking mechanisms, aligning themselves with the sun's trajectory throughout the day to optimize temperature regulation. The mound's materials are meticulously chosen and precisely arranged to maximize insulation and minimize heat loss or gain, representing a remarkable mastery of thermal engineering.

Beyond these well-known examples, countless other insects demonstrate astonishing architectural abilities. Paper wasps construct intricate nests from chewed wood fibres, creating elaborate honeycomb-like structures suspended from branches or eaves. The nests are surprisingly strong and lightweight, demonstrating a remarkable understanding of materials science on a microscopic scale. Carpenter bees bore tunnels into wood, creating sophisticated nesting chambers with partitions to separate their offspring, displaying meticulous craftsmanship and a surprising understanding of spatial organization. Even humble dung beetles, known for their remarkable strength, build intricate balls of dung, using them as both food and shelter for their young, showcasing innovative problem-solving and engineering skills. Their sphere-making, efficient rolling techniques, and clever nest construction deserve a deeper look into their surprisingly sophisticated engineering feats.

The remarkable architectural achievements of insects are not merely isolated instances of natural artistry; they offer valuable insights into diverse fields of science and engineering. Biomimicry, the practice of drawing inspiration from nature to solve human engineering problems, is increasingly utilizing the principles found in insect architecture. The efficiency of honeycomb structures is being applied to the design of lightweight and strong materials, while the self-regulating properties of termite mounds are inspiring the development of innovative building designs focused on energy efficiency and sustainability. The intricate ventilation systems of ant colonies are informing the design of more efficient cooling and air circulation systems. The study of insect architecture is revealing new possibilities for the development of bio-inspired solutions to contemporary challenges in architecture, engineering, and materials science. These miniature architects are not only constructing their own homes; they are shaping the future of human innovation.

The sheer diversity of insect architectural designs, from the simple elegance of a single cell to the complexity of a vast underground city, underscores the power of natural selection and the astonishing adaptability of these creatures. These structures are not only functional; they are also aesthetically pleasing, showcasing a beauty and intricacy that often go unnoticed. The next time you observe a beehive, an ant colony, or a termite mound, take a moment to appreciate the engineering marvel before you, a testament to the ingenuity and complexity of life on Earth. The seemingly simple acts of construction by these insects represent a far more complex process, an ongoing adaptation and response to environmental challenges, a testament to the power of evolution and the surprising sophistication of nature's designs.

The study of insect architecture provides a fascinating glimpse into the intricate world of these often overlooked creatures. It is a field that continues to unveil new discoveries, challenging our assumptions and expanding our understanding of biological innovation. As researchers continue to study these miniature masterpieces, we can expect to uncover even more remarkable insights into the engineering principles at play, leading to new applications in fields ranging from materials science to sustainable design. The insect world, far from being a realm of simple creatures, is a source of unending fascination and inspiration, showcasing the power of natural ingenuity on a scale that is both breathtaking and humbling. The complexity revealed in these miniature structures continues to inspire scientific research, challenge conventional architectural norms and expand our knowledge of the remarkable adaptability of nature.

Furthermore, the sophisticated social structures underlying these architectural feats deserve more attention. The cooperative behaviour and communication systems required to build such complex structures are themselves marvels of evolution. The division of labour, the intricate communication networks, and the seemingly coordinated actions of thousands or even millions of individual insects, all contribute to the success of these collective building projects. The study of these social structures provides insights into the principles of self-organization, emergent behaviour, and the remarkable power of collective intelligence. The intricate interactions between individual insects and the emergent properties of the entire colony are areas of ongoing research, with implications not only for understanding insect societies but also for developing more efficient and robust systems in other fields. The insights gained from studying insect social structures have profound implications for our understanding of complex systems in general, from computer networks to human organizations.

The future of research in insect architecture promises to be even more exciting. Advanced imaging techniques, genetic analysis, and computational modelling are opening new avenues for understanding the complexities of these structures. By combining traditional observation with cutting-edge technology, researchers are gaining unprecedented insights into the mechanisms underlying insect construction, communication, and self-organization. As we delve deeper into the intricacies of insect architecture, we are not only gaining a better understanding of the natural world, but also discovering novel approaches to solving some of humanity's most pressing challenges in engineering, design, and sustainable development. The seemingly simple acts of these minuscule creatures reveal a complexity far exceeding their size, underscoring the immense capacity for innovation found throughout the natural world. The lessons learned from these tiny architects are invaluable, offering a perspective that challenges our preconceived notions about the capabilities of living organisms and the power of collective intelligence.

Unexpected Abilities

LEAVING the intricate world of insect architecture, we now leap into the realm of mammalian marvels, a diverse group boasting an astonishing array of unexpected abilities. Forget the cuddly kittens and playful puppies – the mammalian world is far stranger and more fascinating than you might imagine. We're diving deep into the evolutionary adaptations that have enabled these creatures to thrive in diverse environments, often utilizing strategies that would make even the most seasoned survival expert raise an eyebrow.

Let's start with arguably the most famous mammalian superpower: echolocation. While often associated solely with bats, this remarkable ability isn't exclusive to them. Certain species of dolphins, whales, and even shrews have honed this sophisticated sensory technique to navigate and hunt in environments where sight is limited or unreliable. Imagine a world painted not with light and colour, but with sound – a symphony of echoes revealing the shape, size, and even the texture of objects in complete darkness. These animals emit high-frequency sounds, which bounce off surrounding objects, creating a sonic map in their brains. The precision and speed with which they process this information is breathtaking, allowing them to effortlessly navigate complex underwater environments or pinpoint the location of a tiny insect in a pitch-black cave. This isn't just blind navigation; it's a highly sophisticated form of three-dimensional vision, superior in some respects to our own visual acuity. The complexity of the neural processing involved is currently a hot topic of research, with scientists striving to understand how these animals create such a detailed sonic portrait of their surroundings. The potential applications for this understanding extend far beyond the animal kingdom, offering potential advancements in robotics, navigation systems, and even medical imaging.

But the wonders of mammalian adaptations don't end with echolocation. Consider the remarkable camouflage abilities possessed by various species. The snow leopard, a master of disguise against the stark white backdrop of its Himalayan home, blends seamlessly into its environment, making it nearly invisible to both predator and prey. This isn't simply about coat colour; it's a complex interplay of fur texture, body posture, and even behaviour. The leopard's movements are slow and deliberate, designed to minimize disruption and maintain its camouflage. Similarly, the Arctic fox possesses a remarkable ability to change its fur colour seasonally, transitioning from a snowy white in winter to a mottled brown in summer, perfectly adapting to its ever-changing environment. This chameleon-like adaptation showcases the power of natural selection, allowing these creatures to survive in harsh and unforgiving conditions. The intricate mechanisms behind this fur colour change, involving hormonal signals and pigment cells, continue to intrigue biologists. The study of such adaptive mechanisms provides valuable insights into gene regulation and physiological adaptation, with potential applications in areas such as biomimetic materials and disease treatment.

Moving beyond the visually stunning, let's delve into some less obvious but equally impressive mammalian talents. Take the naked mole-rat, a remarkably unassuming creature that lives in large, highly organized colonies underground. These rodents possess an extraordinary resistance to cancer, a feat that continues to baffle and inspire researchers. Their social structure, characterized by a single reproductive queen and a network of worker castes, presents a fascinating case study in social evolution. Their adaptation to low-oxygen environments is equally impressive, allowing them to survive in oxygen levels that would be fatal to most other mammals. These subterranean dwellers have adapted to a life largely devoid of light, relying on specialized sensory systems and intricate communication strategies to navigate and thrive in their challenging environment. Their resilience, social structure, and unique physiology offer a rich tapestry for scientific inquiry, providing potential insights into cancer research, longevity studies, and the development of new strategies for treating ischemic conditions.

The extraordinary navigational skills of certain mammals are equally astonishing. Many migratory species, like bats and whales, embark on journeys across vast distances, often navigating by the stars, magnetic fields, and other subtle environmental cues. The precision of these journeys, the ability to return to the same breeding grounds year after year, is a testament to their sophisticated navigational abilities and internal compasses. Understanding the mechanisms underlying these impressive feats of navigation is a significant area of research, holding implications for our understanding of animal cognition, sensory perception, and the development of more effective navigation systems. The mechanisms for such complex navigation remain a subject of significant ongoing research, with ongoing studies focusing on possible roles of celestial navigation, magnetic field sensing, and even olfactory cues in these incredible journeys.

Beyond navigation, the remarkable feats of endurance exhibited by certain mammals are worthy of note. The camel, known for its ability to traverse vast deserts with minimal water, is an emblem of resilience. Its physiological adaptations, including its ability to tolerate high body temperatures and conserve water effectively, make it exceptionally well-suited to its arid environment. The study of these adaptations holds significant implications for developing more effective water conservation strategies and enhancing human tolerance to extreme environments. Likewise, the remarkable diving abilities of marine mammals such as seals and whales challenge our understanding of physiological limits. Their ability to withstand immense pressures and extended periods of apnoea is a testament to their incredible adaptations. The study of their physiological systems, particularly their oxygen storage and utilization, has led to new insights into human respiratory physiology and the development of improved diving techniques and medical interventions.

The examples cited represent only a small fraction of the surprising abilities found in the mammalian world. From the electric eels of South America to the echo-locating bats of the tropics, the animal kingdom continuously surprises us with its ingenuity. Each species represents a unique evolutionary trajectory, a testament to the power of natural selection to shape remarkable abilities. The ongoing exploration of these abilities promises not only to expand our knowledge of the natural world but also to inspire innovative solutions to challenges in fields as diverse as medicine, engineering, and computer science. The mammalian world is not merely a collection of cute creatures or potential threats; it is a vast repository of evolutionary innovations waiting to be studied, understood, and admired. It's a source of endless fascination, continually challenging our assumptions and inspiring our imaginations. The ongoing research into these abilities promises a future filled with even more surprising discoveries and a deeper appreciation for the wonder and complexity of the natural world. And that, my friends, is a fact worth celebrating.

Creatures of the Deep

LEAVING the land-lubbing mammals behind, we plunge into the inky blackness of the deep ocean, a realm where the bizarre reigns supreme. Forget your friendly dolphins and playful otters; the abyssal plains are home to creatures so strange they'd make a sci-fi writer blush. We're talking about organisms that have evolved in environments so extreme, so alien to our own experience, that their adaptations are nothing short of miraculous. Pressure that would crush a submarine, perpetual darkness, and a scarcity of food are just a few of the challenges these deep-sea oddballs overcome daily.

Let's start with the angler fish, a creature so wonderfully weird it seems plucked from a nightmare — or perhaps a particularly imaginative episode of "The Twilight Zone." This fish, with its bioluminescent lure dangling enticingly in the darkness, is the epitome of a successful ambush predator. That glowing lure? It's not just a pretty light show; it's a sophisticated hunting tool, attracting unsuspecting prey into the angler fish's gaping maw. And speaking of maws, the angler fish's mouth is disproportionately large, capable of swallowing prey much larger than itself. It's a testament to the power of adaptation in an environment where finding a meal is a constant struggle. They even exhibit sexual parasitism, where the tiny male fuses himself to the much larger female, becoming essentially a living sperm bank. Talk about dedication!

Then there's the vampire squid, a creature so delightfully Gothic its name alone conjures images of shadowy depths and unsettling beauty. But forget the blood-sucking imagery; this cephalopod is far more interesting than its name suggests. Instead of sucking blood, the vampire squid feeds on detritus, essentially marine snow — the slow descent of dead organic matter from the upper ocean. Its dark red colouring, almost black in the deep sea's dim light, provides excellent camouflage. But the true weirdness lies in its unique defence mechanism: when threatened, the vampire squid turns itself inside out, revealing bioluminescent photophores that momentarily dazzle and confuse predators, providing a vital escape window. It's a strategy so unexpectedly elegant, it's hard not to be impressed.

Moving on to the colossal squid, we enter the realm of true giants. While the precise size of these elusive creatures remains a matter of some debate, there's no denying their immense size and frightening appearance. Their enormous eyes, the largest in the animal kingdom, are perfectly adapted to the near-total darkness of their deep-sea habitat. Imagine eyes the size of dinner plates peering back at you from the abyssal depths – a truly terrifying thought. Their massive tentacles, armed with rows of sharp hooks, are used to capture prey, likely a variety of fish and other squids. They're considered a major predator of the deep, a testament to the surprising levels of activity and predation that exist even in the seemingly barren deep ocean.

But the strangeness doesn't stop with the larger creatures. Microscopic life forms in the deep sea also display extraordinary adaptations. Consider the extremophiles, organisms thriving in conditions that would be lethal to most life forms. These microscopic marvels survive and even flourish in scalding hydrothermal vents, places where superheated water spews from the ocean floor, creating chemical gradients that support an entirely unique ecosystem. These creatures, defying our understanding of what life can endure, are a constant reminder of life's remarkable resilience and adaptability.

Consider the barreleye fish, a creature so peculiar it seems straight out of a surrealist painting. Its transparent head allows its tubular eyes to swivel and focus, allowing it to effectively hunt prey both above and below it. This transparency isn't just a neat visual trick; it's a crucial adaptation that maximizes the fish's hunting efficiency.

The deep sea is also home to bioluminescent wonders beyond the angler fish. Many deep-sea creatures use bioluminescence for communication, attracting mates, or luring prey. Some species use it for camouflage, mimicking the faint light filtering down from the surface to avoid detection from predators. This light, produced through complex chemical reactions within the creature's body, paints a spectacular, if largely unseen, light show in the ocean's depths.

Beyond the visually striking, there's the surprising diversity in deep-sea ecosystems. Hydrothermal vents, cold seeps, and whale falls create unique habitats, each supporting a distinct community of specialized organisms. These ecosystems are often characterized by chemosynthesis, a process where organisms derive energy from chemical reactions rather than sunlight, a stark contrast to the photosynthetic ecosystems of the sunlit surface waters.

The exploration of the deep sea is an ongoing adventure, constantly revealing new species and surprising adaptations. Every dive into the abyss is a journey into the unknown, a testament to the vastness and mystery of the ocean and the astonishing diversity of life it harbours. New technologies, such as remotely operated vehicles (ROVs) and autonomous underwater vehicles (AUVs), are continuously expanding our ability to explore these extreme environments, revealing new depths (pun intended) of biological and geological wonder.

Deep-sea exploration also highlights the fragility of these ecosystems. The deep sea, once considered a pristine wilderness, is increasingly affected by human activities, such as deep-sea mining and fishing. Understanding the unique adaptations and delicate balance of these ecosystems is crucial for developing effective conservation strategies to protect these extraordinary creatures and their fragile habitats for future generations. The ongoing research isn't just about cataloguing strange creatures; it's about understanding the intricate web of life that thrives in these extreme environments, and how we can protect it from the increasing impact of human activity.

Even the seemingly simple act of feeding in the deep sea involves fascinating adaptations. Many deep-sea animals are scavengers, feeding on decaying organic matter that sinks from the surface. Some, like the vampire squid mentioned earlier, specialize in consuming marine snow, while others scavenge on the carcasses of larger animals, often whales that have sunk to the ocean floor, creating localized "whale falls" that support entire ecosystems. These whale falls, in a sense, are underwater oases, providing a concentrated source of food in an otherwise sparse environment.

The deep sea also offers a unique window into evolutionary history. Many deep-sea organisms represent ancient lineages, having evolved in relative isolation for millions of years. Studying these organisms can provide invaluable insights into the history of life on Earth, revealing evolutionary pathways and adaptations that have shaped the biodiversity of our planet. The deep sea is, in essence, a living museum of evolutionary history, a testament to the incredible resilience and adaptability of life.

The discovery of new deep-sea species is a regular occurrence. Every expedition seems to uncover creatures with bizarre adaptations and unusual morphologies, continually challenging our understanding of life's diversity. These discoveries emphasize the need for ongoing research and exploration, ensuring that we continue to uncover the secrets of this fascinating and largely unexplored realm. The abyss remains a place of mystery and wonder, a constant source of fascination for scientists and enthusiasts alike. And, as our technology continues to advance, we can look forward to even more remarkable discoveries in the years to come, further expanding our knowledge of the ocean's depths and the astonishing creatures that call them home.

In the face of the vast unknown, the deep sea remains a stark reminder of the incredible diversity and resilience of life on Earth. From the bioluminescent wonders to the pressure-adapted giants, the ocean's depths are a testament to the power of natural selection to sculpt life into breathtaking and often bizarre forms. It's a world that challenges our assumptions about what life can be, pushing the boundaries of our understanding of biology and ecology. The ongoing exploration of this realm promises to continue unveiling astonishing facts and breathtaking discoveries for years to come, reminding us that the most extraordinary wonders often lie hidden in the deepest, darkest places.

Ancient Wisdom
Modern Myths

SLITHERING out of the ocean's depths and onto drier land, we encounter a group of creatures often misunderstood and frequently maligned: reptiles. Far from the scaly villains of countless horror films, the reptilian world is a dazzling tapestry of evolutionary innovation, boasting a diversity that belies their often-stereotyped image. Let's shed some light on these fascinating creatures, debunking common myths and uncovering some truly astonishing facts.

Did you know that some snakes can "hear" through their jaws? It's true! While they lack external ears, certain species, like the pit vipers, possess highly sensitive heat-detecting pits near their mouths. These pits allow them to sense the subtle infrared radiation emitted by warm-blooded prey, effectively "hearing" their movements even in complete darkness. This remarkable adaptation highlights the incredible ways in which animals can evolve to exploit their environment, even in seemingly insurmountable circumstances. The evolution of these heat-sensing organs is a perfect example of natural selection at work, a constant refinement driven by the relentless pressure of survival.

The chameleon, another well-known reptilian marvel, is often associated with its color-changing abilities. But what exactly is going on when a chameleon shifts its hues? It's not a matter of camouflage in the way we typically understand it. Chameleons change colour to communicate! Different colour combinations convey moods and intentions—think of it as a sophisticated reptilian form of nonverbal communication. They adjust their colour based on factors like temperature, light levels, and even their emotional state. The vibrant shifts aren't solely for hiding; they're a dynamic visual language. Recent research has even shown that the intricate cellular structure of their skin plays a crucial role in this complex process, with specialized pigment-containing cells working in concert to create the stunning shifts in appearance. This sophisticated system is a far cry from the simplistic notion of camouflage, revealing a level of complexity that is frequently overlooked.

Speaking of communication, the hissing of a cobra isn't just a random noise. It's a carefully controlled expulsion of air, a warning signal, and a remarkable display of intimidation. The sound itself is produced by forcing air through its nostrils, creating a characteristic hiss that can be surprisingly loud and effective in deterring potential threats. This isn't simply a reflexive reaction, but a sophisticated behaviour honed over millions of years of evolution. The cobra's hood, a distensible neck flap, only adds to the dramatic effect, making the reptile appear larger and more menacing. This impressive display is a perfect example of how natural selection favours traits that enhance survival and reproductive success, even when those traits seem frightening to us.

Moving beyond the charismatic reptiles, let's consider the less-celebrated, but equally fascinating, tuatara. This ancient reptile, found only in New Zealand, is often described as a "living fossil." Its lineage stretches back to the time of the dinosaurs, and its unique biology has intrigued scientists for centuries. The tuatara possesses a third eye, a parietal eye, situated on the top of its head. This eye is not fully developed for vision like our two eyes, but it is light-sensitive and plays a role in regulating the animal's circadian rhythms and thermoregulation. It serves as a testament to the remarkable resilience of certain lineages, surviving mass extinction events and retaining features that have long since disappeared in other branches of the reptilian family tree. Its existence is a tangible link to a distant past. Their slow metabolism and longevity, exceeding a century in some cases, further enhance their mystique and add to the ongoing research interest in their unique evolutionary path.

The diversity of reptile scales also deserves attention. While often viewed as simply protective armour, reptile scales are incredibly diverse in structure, texture, and function. Some are smooth and overlapping, offering protection from abrasion; others are keeled and spiny, providing additional defence against predators. The coloration and patterning of scales also play a crucial role in camouflage, thermoregulation, and communication. The complexity of scale structure and the subtle variations between species reflect the remarkable adaptability of these creatures to a wide range of habitats and ecological niches. Understanding these differences provides valuable insights into the evolutionary relationships between different reptilian groups.

The reproductive strategies of reptiles are equally diverse and fascinating. Some reptiles lay eggs, while others give birth to live young. Even amongst egg-laying species, there's a spectrum of parental care, ranging from no care whatsoever to extensive incubation and protection of the offspring. This variation reflects the enormous diversity of environments in which reptiles have evolved, with different reproductive strategies being favoured depending on the specific environmental pressures faced by each species. The adaptive landscape of reptile reproduction is a dynamic and intricate phenomenon that constantly reminds us of the complexity of evolutionary processes. The strategies employed are not merely a matter of chance but a reflection of millions of years of adaptation and refinement.

Now, let's dispel a few common myths about reptiles. Contrary to popular belief, not all reptiles are cold-blooded. While many reptiles are ectothermic, meaning they rely on external sources of heat to regulate their body temperature, some species, such as some larger snakes and marine iguanas, exhibit a degree of endothermy, being able to generate internal heat, especially during activity. This highlights the complexity and nuance of the classification schemes used in biology, reminding us that nature doesn't always fit neatly into pre-defined boxes. The lines between "cold-blooded" and "warm-blooded" are often blurry in the reptile kingdom.

Another misconception is that all reptiles are dangerous. While some reptiles, such as venomous snakes and certain lizards, pose a risk to humans, the vast majority are harmless and play crucial roles in their ecosystems. Many reptiles help control populations of insects and other invertebrates, preventing ecological imbalances. Others serve as a vital food source for larger predators, maintaining the intricate web of life within their respective habitats. Fear and prejudice often overshadow the essential roles that reptiles play in the maintenance of global biodiversity. Appreciating their ecological significance is vital to effective conservation efforts.

The evolution of venomous reptiles is a fascinating story of adaptation and co-evolution. Venom is a complex cocktail of proteins and other substances, each tailored to subdue prey or deter predators. The evolution of venom delivery systems, ranging from grooved fangs to hollow needles, is also a remarkable feat of evolutionary engineering. Venom systems have evolved independently in several reptilian lineages, highlighting the power of convergent evolution – the process whereby unrelated organisms develop similar traits in response to similar selective pressures. This arms race between predator and prey, with each evolving countermeasures and adaptations, is a captivating example of the dynamism of natural selection.

Reptiles have a long and often misunderstood history intertwined with human culture. From ancient Egyptian mythology to modern folklore, reptiles have held various symbolic meanings in societies worldwide. Some cultures revere them as symbols of wisdom, power, or even divinity, while others view them with fear and superstition. These varied interpretations reflect the complex and multifaceted relationship between humans and reptiles, a relationship that has often been defined by both fascination and fear. The study of the cultural representations of reptiles offers valuable insights into human beliefs, values, and the ways in which we interact with the natural world. Understanding these cultural perceptions is crucial for shaping responsible and ethical interactions with reptile populations.

Finally, the conservation status of many reptile species is of growing concern. Habitat loss, climate change, and the illegal wildlife trade pose significant threats to countless reptile populations worldwide. Many species are facing extinction, and the loss of these animals would have far-reaching consequences for the ecosystems they inhabit. Protecting reptile populations is not merely a matter of preserving biodiversity; it is essential for maintaining the health and stability of entire ecosystems and preserving our planet's natural heritage. The ongoing work of herpetologists and conservation organizations is crucial in mitigating these threats and ensuring the survival of these remarkable creatures for generations to come. Their efforts serve as a crucial reminder of our responsibility to protect the biodiversity of our planet. The future of reptiles, and indeed the future of the planet, depends on our willingness to engage in responsible conservation practices.

A Surprisingly Complex Fruit

BANANAS. Those ubiquitous, potassium-packed curves of yellow goodness. Seemingly simple, right? Wrong! The humble banana harbours a surprising depth of scientific complexity, a veritable cornucopia of botanical brilliance, and a surprisingly fascinating history. Let's peel back the layers (pun intended) and delve into the surprisingly complex world of the banana.

First, let's address the obvious: the shape. That iconic crescent moon isn't just aesthetically pleasing; it's a marvel of evolutionary engineering. The curve isn't arbitrary; it's an optimization for efficient sunlight absorption. The slightly curved shape allows for more even exposure to the sun's rays during its growth, maximizing photosynthesis and resulting in a more efficiently produced fruit. Think of it as nature's own solar panel, cleverly designed for optimal energy harvesting.

But the shape isn't the only ingenious aspect of banana design. Consider the peel. That seemingly simple outer layer is a complex structure composed of multiple layers, each with its own specific function. These layers provide protection from pests, disease, and the elements, ensuring the delicate inner fruit reaches maturity safely. The peel's ability to withstand significant physical stress – think of those bananas jostling in the supermarket – is a testament to its robust engineering. The peel also plays a crucial role in the ripening process, releasing ethylene gas that signals the transition from green to yellow, signalling the delicious, edible stage.

Speaking of ripening, the banana's transformation from a firm, green fruit to its soft, yellow counterpart is a complex biochemical process. This change is driven by enzymes that break down starch into sugars, resulting in the sweet flavour we all know and love. The precise timing and orchestration of this enzymatic activity are remarkable feats of biological engineering, ensuring the fruit achieves optimal edibility at the right time. And the browning that occurs after the peak of ripeness? That's a result of oxidation, a chemical reaction that causes the enzymes to further react and change the colour. It doesn't necessarily mean the banana is inedible, though! It can still be delicious in many baked goods, where its sweet flavour will shine.

Beyond its physical attributes, the banana's genetic makeup is equally fascinating. The Cavendish banana, the most commonly consumed variety globally, is, ironically, a clone. Almost all Cavendish bananas are genetically identical, a result of extensive cultivation and propagation. This lack of genetic diversity is a double-edged sword. On one hand, it ensures consistent quality and flavour, delighting consumers globally. On the other hand, it makes the Cavendish banana incredibly vulnerable to diseases. A single pathogen could wipe out the entire global crop, highlighting the fragility of monoculture.

The banana's journey from field to table is also a testament to human ingenuity and global trade networks. Bananas grown in tropical regions are shipped around the world, requiring sophisticated transportation and storage methods to maintain quality. The process is a fascinating blend of agricultural science, logistics, and international cooperation. Consider the environmental impact of this process, too. The carbon footprint associated with banana transport across continents is considerable, raising questions about sustainability and the need for more localized food production.

Moreover, the banana is far more than just a source of dietary potassium. Its composition is a treasure trove of various vitamins and minerals. In addition to potassium, it contains a good source of vitamin B6, vitamin C, and fibre. These nutrients contribute to overall health and well-being, making the banana a powerhouse of nutrition. It's no wonder that the banana has secured its place as a staple food item around the world and is even used in many countries to provide essential nutrients to children.

Furthermore, the banana's impact extends beyond the nutritional. It's played a significant role in the cultural landscapes of many nations. From its appearances in pop culture to its use in folklore and traditional practices, it transcends its role as a simple fruit. Consider, for instance, the famous banana republic concept: a term used to describe politically unstable countries dependent on export economies, and often associated with banana production. This highlights the historical connection between the banana and socio-political dynamics in many nations.

Beyond the widely known varieties, the world of bananas is incredibly diverse. There exists a staggering number of banana cultivars, each with unique characteristics and flavours. Some are sweet, others tangy; some are small, others massive; and the colours range beyond the familiar yellow, encompassing red, green, and even almost-black varieties. This diversity underscores the botanical complexity of the banana plant.

The seemingly simple banana, therefore, unveils a surprising wealth of scientific wonders. Its unique shape, its complex peel, its fascinating ripening process, its genetic homogeneity, its global transport, its nutritional contributions, and its cultural significance all combine to create a profile far richer and more intricate than one might initially suspect. Next time you peel a banana, take a moment to appreciate the complex interplay of science, history, and culture that has brought this seemingly simple fruit to your hand. It's a reminder that even the most mundane things in our lives often possess a surprisingly complex and intriguing story to tell. And this, my friends, is why bananas are far from boring! The journey of a banana from seed to supermarket shelf is a fascinating tale of biological processes, global trade, and culinary history. From its origins in the tropical forests of Southeast Asia, it has become a global commodity, enjoyed by billions worldwide. The complexities of the banana – its growth, its propagation, its ripening, and its distribution – are all testaments to the interconnectedness of our world. Each banana we consume is the result of a complex interplay of nature and human intervention, a fascinating confluence of scientific knowledge and cultural significance.

Mysteries of the Subatomic World

LEAVING the wonderfully weird world of bananas behind, we now enter a realm far stranger, a place where logic takes a holiday and common sense goes on an extended vacation: the subatomic world of quantum mechanics. Forget everything you think you know about how things work, because at the quantum level, the rules are…different. Let's just say, if reality had a rebellious teenage phase, this is it.

Imagine a world where a particle can be in multiple places at once – like a mischievous ghost flitting between rooms – a phenomenon known as superposition. It's not just a theoretical quirk either; experiments have demonstrably shown this bizarre behaviour. Think of it as a cosmic game of hide-and-seek, where the particle is simultaneously hiding and found, existing in a probabilistic haze until we try to observe it. This brings us to another head-scratcher: the observer effect. The very act of measuring a quantum system seemingly forces it to "choose" a state. It's as if the universe only makes up its mind about the reality of a particle when we decide to look!

Then there's entanglement, a mind-bending phenomenon where two particles become linked, regardless of the distance separating them. Change the state of one, and instantly, the other changes, too. Einstein famously called it "spooky action at a distance," and with good reason. This instantaneous connection seems to defy the speed of light, a fundamental cosmic speed limit. It's as if these particles are communicating faster than information could possibly travel, a clear violation of our classical understanding of causality. Imagine two coins flipped simultaneously, and no matter how far apart they are, they always land on the same side – heads or tails. That's the essence of entanglement, though considerably more complex and far less simplistic than a mere coin flip.

These quantum oddities aren't just theoretical musings confined to dusty physics textbooks. They have very real-world implications, and it is precisely that that makes them so fascinating. Quantum mechanics is the bedrock of many technologies we use daily. Laser scanners at the grocery store, the MRI machines in hospitals, and the very transistors in our computers – all rely on the principles of quantum mechanics to function. This technology, which is intrinsically linked to the strange quantum world, continues to be developed at an exponential rate, further blurring the lines between what is observed and what is understood.

The implications extend far beyond the technological. Our understanding of reality itself is being challenged by quantum mechanics. The very concept of causality, the notion that one event directly causes another, is brought into question. The universe at the quantum level appears less like a clockwork mechanism and more like a cosmic dice game, ruled by probability rather than unwavering determinism. It's a disconcerting thought, but also thrilling. It suggests that our universe is far more nuanced and complex than we ever previously imagined.

Consider the infamous Schrödinger's cat thought experiment. A cat is placed in a box with a radioactive atom. If the atom decays, a mechanism triggers the release of poison, killing the cat. According to quantum mechanics, until we open the box and observe the system, the atom exists in a superposition of decayed and undecayed states, meaning the cat is simultaneously both alive and dead. It's a paradox that highlights the absurdity of applying classical logic to quantum phenomena, demonstrating the limitations of our everyday understanding of reality.

Further complicating matters is the measurement problem. How does the act of observation collapse the superposition and force a particle to "choose" a state? Various interpretations have been proposed, some suggesting that consciousness plays a role, others proposing alternative explanations that do not involve conscious observation. The debate continues, fuelling ongoing research and philosophical discussions on the nature of reality and the role of the observer.

Beyond the philosophical quandaries, the practical applications of quantum mechanics continue to evolve. Quantum computing, for instance, promises to revolutionize various fields by leveraging the principles of superposition and entanglement to perform computations far beyond the capabilities of classical computers. Imagine computers capable of solving problems currently deemed intractable, breaking even the most advanced encryption, or simulating complex molecular interactions for the development of new drugs and materials.

Quantum cryptography offers the potential for unbreakable encryption methods, a game-changer in the realm of cybersecurity. By using the principles of quantum mechanics, information can be secured in ways that are theoretically impervious to hacking, relying on the very laws of physics to safeguard sensitive data. Quantum sensors are also on the rise, offering unparalleled precision in various applications, ranging from medical imaging to navigation systems and environmental monitoring.

Yet, the journey to unlocking the full potential of quantum mechanics is far from over. Many fundamental questions remain unanswered. What exactly is the nature of wave-particle duality? How do we reconcile the probabilistic nature of quantum mechanics with the deterministic world we experience on a macroscopic scale? What are the limits of quantum entanglement, and how can we harness its power more effectively? These are some of the significant mysteries that continue to fuel the intense research in quantum physics, propelling us forward in our understanding of the universe at its most fundamental level.

The strangeness of the quantum world, however, is not a sign of its incomprehensibility, but rather a testament to its profound depth and complexity. It is a reminder that our intuition, honed by our everyday experiences in the macroscopic world, fails to grasp the subtle intricacies of the subatomic realm. The counter-intuitive nature of quantum mechanics is not a flaw in our understanding, but rather a reflection of the universe's inherent strangeness – a universe that is far more bewildering and beautiful than our classical models could ever have suggested.

As we venture deeper into the quantum realm, we must abandon our preconceived notions of how things "should" work. We must embrace the inherent probabilistic nature of the universe, accepting that randomness and uncertainty are not flaws but fundamental aspects of reality. The quantum world offers not just scientific breakthroughs, but a fundamental re-evaluation of our place in the cosmos and the very nature of existence itself. It is a world of paradoxes and probabilities, a place where logic bends and reality itself seems to shimmer and waver. But it is also a world brimming with potential, a world that holds the key to unlocking technologies and insights that could transform our lives in ways we can only begin to imagine. So next time you marvel at the workings of your computer or the precision of an MRI scan, remember the bizarre, beautiful, and undeniably strange world of quantum mechanics – a testament to the universe's boundless capacity to surprise and amaze.

The exploration of quantum mechanics is ongoing, a constant push to refine our models and further unravel the mysteries of the subatomic world. Each new discovery brings us closer to a deeper understanding of the fundamental building blocks of reality, while simultaneously highlighting the vast expanse of the unknown that still remains. This constant evolution is what makes the study of quantum mechanics such a vibrant and intellectually stimulating field. It's not merely a collection of facts and figures, but a dynamic and ever-evolving landscape of knowledge, a frontier of discovery that stretches far into the future.

The sheer audacity of quantum theory challenges our deeply ingrained notions of causality and determinism. The notion that the act of observation affects the reality of a particle is not just counter-intuitive, it shakes the very foundations of our understanding of the universe. It forces us to question the very nature of reality itself, pushing us to explore alternative models and interpretations, each bringing its own set of insights and challenges.

Quantum entanglement, in particular, stands as a remarkable example of the universe's ability to defy our expectations. The instantaneous correlation between entangled particles, regardless of the distance separating them, hints at a level of interconnectedness far beyond our classical understanding. This phenomenon continues to be a source of both fascination and confusion, spurring on new experiments and interpretations that aim to shed light on this remarkable property of the quantum world. Its exploration promises to reveal deeper insights into the nature of space, time, and the fundamental forces that govern our universe.

The future of quantum mechanics holds untold potential for technological advancement and scientific discovery. Quantum computing, while still in its relative infancy, has the potential to revolutionize fields ranging from medicine and materials science to artificial intelligence and cryptography. The possibilities seem limitless, and the ongoing race to develop functional and robust quantum computers is a testament to the transformative potential of this field. With each advance, we inch closer to a future where quantum technologies become integral parts of our daily lives. But the exploration of quantum mechanics also holds a deeper significance. It challenges our fundamental understanding of the universe and our place within it, forcing us to confront the limitations of our intuition and the vastness of the unknown. It is a journey of discovery, a quest to unveil the deepest mysteries of reality itself, a testament to the ongoing human endeavour to understand the cosmos. It is, to borrow a phrase, a quantum leap in our understanding, a truly breathtaking journey that promises many surprises yet to come.

A Rainbow
of Reactions

FROM the bizarre quantum realm, we now shift our gaze to something a bit more... grounded, though no less fascinating: colour. We perceive colour every day, from the vibrant hues of a sunset to the subtle shades of a forest, yet the science behind these captivating visual experiences is surprisingly complex and utterly captivating. It's a world where electrons dance, photons leap, and the very nature of light determines the spectacle we witness. Forget the simple rainbow mnemonic — the true chemistry of colour is far more nuanced and, dare we say, far more entertaining.

The foundation of our perception of colour lies in light itself. Light, as we learned in school (and hopefully remember!), is electromagnetic radiation. This radiation spans a vast spectrum, from the incredibly long wavelengths of radio waves to the infinitesimally short wavelengths of gamma rays. The visible spectrum, the tiny sliver of this electromagnetic range that our eyes can detect, is what we perceive as colour. Within this narrow band, different wavelengths correspond to different colours. Longer wavelengths appear reddish, while shorter wavelengths appear bluish. This seemingly simple relationship forms the basis for an astonishing array of colour phenomena.

Now, let's delve into the chemical reactions that paint our world in such vivid shades. The colours we see in most objects aren't actually produced by the object itself; instead, they're a result of how the object interacts with light. Think about a red apple. The apple doesn't "create" red light; it absorbs all wavelengths of light except red, which it reflects back to our eyes. This selective absorption and reflection of light is determined by the chemical composition of the apple's skin, specifically the presence of certain pigments.

Pigments are essentially light-absorbing molecules. These molecules possess specific electron configurations that allow them to absorb certain wavelengths of light and reflect others. The specific wavelengths absorbed and reflected determine the colour we perceive. For instance, chlorophyll, the pigment that makes plants green, absorbs most wavelengths of light except green, which it reflects. That's why plants appear green to us!

The diversity of colours in nature and the objects we create is a testament to the immense variety of pigment molecules. Consider the vibrant blues of sapphires, the fiery reds of rubies, or the dazzling yellows of sunflowers. Each colour arises from the unique chemical structure of the pigment involved. Sapphires owe their blue hue to trace amounts of titanium and iron within their aluminium oxide crystal structure. These impurities subtly alter the crystal's electronic properties, leading to the selective absorption and reflection of light that produces the stunning blue colour. Rubies, on the other hand, get their crimson glow from chromium ions embedded within their corundum structure. The chromium ions absorb green and blue light, leaving the red light to be reflected. This is not just simple reflection, but a complex dance of electrons absorbing and emitting photons – a light show at the molecular level.

Let's venture into the world of synthetic pigments, the colourful chemicals that bring life to paints, dyes, and inks. Many of these pigments are organic compounds, meaning they're carbon-based molecules with complex structures. The arrangement of atoms within these molecules significantly impacts their light-absorbing properties. Slight changes in molecular structure can dramatically alter the colour of the pigment. This ability to manipulate colour through molecular design has revolutionized industries ranging from fashion and cosmetics to art and construction.

Take the azo dyes, a hugely important class of synthetic pigments. These dyes, often used to colour fabrics, are characterized by the presence of a nitrogen-nitrogen double bond, known as an azo group (-N=N-). The azo group is responsible for many of the dye's colour-producing properties. By modifying the substituents attached to the azo group – think of them as colourful decorations on a molecular skeleton – chemists can fine-tune the dye's light absorption, creating a breathtaking array of colours. This control over colour synthesis is remarkable, allowing the creation of dyes that span the entire visible spectrum and beyond.

Furthermore, the chemical environment can significantly influence the colour of a substance. The pH of a solution, for instance, can alter the colour of certain indicators. Litmus paper, a classic example, changes colour depending on the acidity or basicity of the solution it's dipped into. This colour change is a result of the chemical transformation of the litmus indicator molecule in response to changes in pH. In acidic conditions, the molecule adopts one form, absorbing certain wavelengths and reflecting others, resulting in a red colour. In basic conditions, the molecule undergoes a structural change, shifting its light absorption properties and resulting in a blue colour. It's a molecular chameleon, its colour shifting depending on its chemical surroundings.

Another fascinating example of the chemical influence on colour is found in the phenomenon of fluorescence. Certain molecules, called fluorophores, absorb light at one wavelength and then re-emit light at a longer wavelength. This process, known as fluorescence, can result in vibrant and often unexpected colours. Fluorescent pigments are used extensively in highlighter pens, clothing, and even biological imaging. The specific colour of fluorescence depends on the molecular structure of the fluorophore, making it possible to create highly specific fluorescent dyes for a wide range of applications. Imagine a world without those brightly coloured highlighters – the very thought is almost painful!

But the chemistry of colour extends beyond pigments and dyes. The structural coloration found in many natural materials, such as butterfly wings or peacock feathers, is not due to pigments but rather to the intricate microstructure of the material itself. These structures, often consisting of layered or regularly spaced components, interact with light in ways that produce intense and iridescent colours. This type of coloration is a mesmerizing display of physics and chemistry working in harmony to create visual splendour. These intricate structures diffract and interfere with light waves, causing certain wavelengths to be amplified while others are suppressed, leading to brilliant and often shifting colours. Think of the shimmering iridescence of an oil slick – that's structural coloration at play!

The captivating aspect of structural coloration is its ability to produce colours that are independent of the chemical composition of the material itself. This means that similar colours can be produced from materials with vastly different chemical make-ups, as long as the microstructure is properly organized. This phenomenon has inspired numerous biomimetic efforts, attempts to mimic nature's ingenious designs to create new materials and technologies with enhanced optical properties. The potential applications range from improved displays and coatings to advanced camouflage and sensing technologies. Nature, once again, provides us with a blueprint for innovation.

Even the colour of our own skin, a seemingly simple observation, is a complex interplay of chemistry. Melanin, the pigment responsible for skin colour, is produced by specialized cells called melanocytes. The amount and type of melanin produced determine our skin tone, ranging from very light to very dark. This variation is influenced by genetic factors, sun exposure, and other environmental factors. Melanin's primary function is to protect the skin from the harmful effects of ultraviolet (UV) radiation, highlighting the vital role of chemical processes in our very existence. The production and distribution of melanin illustrate how complex chemical interactions translate to visible traits, revealing the intricate link between our chemistry and our outward appearance.

And so, the seemingly simple question of "why is this thing this colour?" Opens a window into a fascinating world of chemical reactions, molecular structures, and light interactions. It reveals a story that intertwines the fundamental laws of physics with the intricacies of molecular chemistry, producing a spectacular array of colours that enrich our lives and challenge our understanding of the natural world. From the vibrant hues of a tropical rainforest to the subtle shades of a desert landscape, colour is a testament to the breathtaking power of chemistry, a vibrant and ever-evolving story unfolded through light and molecules. So, the next time you admire a sunset or a flower, remember the incredible chemical dance happening behind the scenes, a microscopic symphony of light and molecules that brings the beauty of the world into clear, vibrant, and unforgettable focus.

Universes
of Wonders

OUR journey from the microscopic marvels of colour now takes us on a colossal leap – quite literally – into the vast, awe-inspiring expanse of the cosmos. Prepare for a mind-bending exploration of celestial secrets, where the scale is so immense, and the phenomena so bizarre, that even the most imaginative science fiction writer would struggle to keep up.

Let's start with something seemingly simple: size. We're used to thinking in terms of kilometres, maybe miles, perhaps even light-years for the truly ambitious. But when contemplating the universe, even light-years pale into insignificance. The observable universe, the portion we can currently detect, is estimated to be around 93 billion light-years in diameter. That's 93 billion years that light would take to travel across it, travelling at an astounding speed of 186,000 miles per second. To put that into perspective, imagine trying to count to 93 billion – you'd be counting for a very, very long time. And that's just the part we can see. What lies beyond remains a tantalizing mystery, a cosmic enigma wrapped in a veil of darkness and distance.

The sheer scale of the universe is almost incomprehensible. Consider this: every speck of light you see in the night sky – each tiny pinprick of brilliance – is a sun, often far larger and more massive than our own. Some of these stars boast planetary systems of their own, potentially teeming with worlds we can only dream of. The probability of Earth being the only planet harbouring life within this vast cosmic ocean seems statistically improbable, bordering on absurd. The sheer number of stars is staggering; our own Milky Way galaxy alone contains hundreds of billions, perhaps even trillions, each a potential sun with its own retinue of planets. And our galaxy is just one among billions, maybe trillions, of others within the observable universe. This is the mind-boggling truth of cosmic immensity.

Now, let's delve into the truly bizarre: black holes. These cosmic behemoths are regions of space-time where gravity is so incredibly strong that nothing, not even light, can escape their grasp. They are born from the catastrophic collapse of massive stars, their cores imploding under their own immense weight. Imagine a star many times larger than our sun, collapsing into a point of infinite density – a singularity – creating a gravitational well so deep that even time itself is warped and distorted around it.

The event horizon, the boundary beyond which no escape is possible, is a point of no return. Anything crossing it, from asteroids to entire stars, is destined to be crushed and absorbed into the singularity. The gravitational forces at the event horizon are so extreme that they would spaghettify anything unfortunate enough to approach, stretching it out into an incredibly long, thin strand. Not exactly a comfortable prospect.

Black holes are more than just cosmic vacuum cleaners; they play a crucial role in the evolution of galaxies. Their immense gravity influences the movement and distribution of stars and gas within a galaxy. In fact, super-massive black holes, millions or even billions of times more massive than our sun, are thought to reside at the heart of most galaxies, acting as galactic anchors. These behemoths hold the key to understanding galactic structure and evolution.

The search for extraterrestrial life is another captivating aspect of our cosmic exploration. Given the sheer scale of the universe, the possibility of life existing beyond Earth seems increasingly likely. Scientists are actively searching for biosignatures, indicators of life, in the atmospheres of exoplanets, planets orbiting stars other than our sun. They are looking for gases like oxygen, methane, and water vapour, which could be evidence of biological activity.

The Kepler space telescope, and more recently the TESS (Transiting Exoplanet Survey Satellite) mission, have been instrumental in discovering thousands of exoplanets, many of which reside within the habitable zones of their stars – the region where liquid water, a crucial ingredient for life as we know it, could exist on the surface. The search for extraterrestrial intelligence (SETI) takes a different approach, listening for radio signals from other civilizations, hoping to detect deliberate attempts at interstellar communication. While we haven't yet found definitive proof of alien life, the search continues, fuelled by the tantalizing possibility of discovering life beyond Earth, potentially altering our understanding of our place in the cosmos.

Beyond black holes and exoplanets, the universe offers a plethora of other wonders. Pulsars, rapidly rotating neutron stars, emit beams of electromagnetic radiation that sweep across the sky like cosmic lighthouses. Quasars, incredibly luminous objects powered by super-massive black holes, are among the most distant and energetic objects in the universe. Nebulae, vast clouds of gas and dust, are stellar nurseries where new stars are born. Each of these celestial phenomena offers a glimpse into the magnificent complexity and grandeur of the cosmos.

Our understanding of the universe is constantly evolving. New discoveries and advancements in technology continuously challenge our existing knowledge and push the boundaries of our understanding. With each new observation, we inch closer to unravelling the universe's deepest secrets, from the formation of galaxies to the origin of life itself.

The universe, in all its vastness and complexity, is a testament to the power of scientific inquiry. From the smallest subatomic particle to the largest galactic structures, the cosmos presents us with endless opportunities for discovery and wonder. The mysteries that remain far outweigh the answers we've uncovered, and that's precisely what makes the exploration of the universe such a compelling and awe-inspiring endeavour. The humbling scale of the cosmos puts our own existence, our triumphs and tribulations, into a remarkable perspective. We are a tiny speck, a fleeting moment in the grand tapestry of cosmic time. Yet, we are also capable of marvelling at the universe's magnificence, capable of exploring its secrets, and capable of seeking answers to the biggest questions humanity has ever pondered.

The ongoing search for answers to questions about the universe's origins, its evolution, and the potential for life beyond Earth drives scientific innovation and fosters international collaboration. Projects like the James Webb Space Telescope, with its unprecedented ability to observe the universe in infrared light, are pushing the frontiers of astronomical observation, revealing details of distant galaxies and exoplanets never before seen. This pursuit of knowledge extends beyond the realm of pure science, fostering a sense of wonder and inspiring future generations of scientists and explorers.

The exploration of space also carries profound philosophical implications. The sheer scale of the universe challenges anthropocentric viewpoints and encourages us to consider our place in the cosmic scheme. This vastness emphasizes the interconnectedness of everything and the delicate balance of life on Earth. The universe's age, measured in billions of years, compels us to contemplate the vastness of time and the relative brevity of human existence, fostering a sense of perspective and appreciation for the preciousness of life.

In addition to the scientific discoveries and philosophical reflections, space exploration has also generated numerous technological advancements with practical applications in our daily lives. The technologies developed for space missions—from materials science and computing to communication and navigation—have led to innovations that improve our lives on Earth. These spin-off technologies demonstrate the significant economic and societal benefits of investing in space research.

The mysteries of the universe continue to captivate and inspire. From the enigmatic nature of dark matter and dark energy, which constitute the vast majority of the universe's mass-energy density, to the possibility of parallel universes or the existence of multi-verses, the universe presents countless unanswered questions. These mysteries not only drive scientific inquiry but also fuel our imagination and inspire a sense of wonder about the cosmos.

Furthermore, our understanding of celestial mechanics has expanded dramatically over the centuries. Early astronomers developed sophisticated models of planetary motion, culminating in Kepler's laws and Newton's theory of universal gravitation. Einstein's theory of general relativity revolutionized our understanding of gravity, revealing its connection to the curvature of space-time. The discovery of cosmic microwave background radiation provided crucial evidence supporting the Big Bang theory, the prevailing cosmological model that explains the universe's origins and evolution. Each of these milestones represents a triumph of human intellect and ingenuity, pushing the boundaries of our knowledge and understanding.

The ongoing exploration of the cosmos requires international cooperation and collaboration. Large-scale projects, such as the International Space Station and the Square Kilometre Array radio telescope, are prime examples of this global partnership in science. These collaborations highlight the shared human desire to understand the universe and demonstrate the power of international cooperation in addressing global challenges. The sharing of knowledge and resources fosters a sense of global community and accelerates scientific progress.

As we conclude this exploration of the universe's wonders, let us remember that our journey of discovery is far from over. The universe continues to unfold its secrets, offering countless opportunities for future exploration and discovery. With every new observation and each technological advancement, we move closer to unravelling the universe's enigmatic mysteries and gaining a deeper understanding of our place within this grand and awe-inspiring cosmic realm. The cosmos is a source of endless wonder, inspiring awe, curiosity, and a profound appreciation for the universe's breathtaking scale and complexity. The journey continues, and with each step forward, the universe reveals more of its astounding secrets.

The Surprising World of Cells

FROM the cosmic vastness, we now shrink our focus to the incredibly intricate world within—the microscopic battlegrounds and breathtaking collaborations happening inside every single cell in our bodies. It's a realm of constant activity, a bustling metropolis teeming with molecular machinery and intricate processes that make life itself possible. Think of it as a tiny, self-contained city, complete with its own power plants (mitochondria), waste disposal systems (lysosomes), and even its own intricate communication networks. But this cellular city isn't always perfectly run; sometimes, things go spectacularly wrong, leading to fascinating biological blunders that are almost comical in their unintended consequences.

Let's start with the power plants, the mitochondria. These are often referred to as the "powerhouses of the cell," and rightly so. They're responsible for generating the energy that fuels all cellular processes. But these powerhouses aren't perfect. Mitochondrial dysfunction, resulting from mutations or environmental factors, can lead to a range of diseases, from mild fatigue to debilitating conditions like mitochondrial myopathy. Imagine a city-wide power outage – that's essentially what happens in the cell when these power plants malfunction. The consequences can be dramatic, highlighting the crucial role mitochondria play in maintaining cellular health.

The intricacies of cellular communication are equally remarkable. Cells constantly communicate with each other, exchanging signals and coordinating their activities. This communication is essential for everything from tissue development to immune responses. However, errors in communication can lead to serious problems. For example, uncontrolled cell growth, a hallmark of cancer, can result from faulty signalling pathways. In a way, it's like a city where the communication systems break down, leading to chaos and uncontrolled expansion.

Then there are the cellular garbage disposals, the lysosomes. These organelles are responsible for breaking down waste products and cellular debris. If the lysosomes malfunction, waste can build up inside the cell, leading to various diseases, including lysosomal storage disorders. Picture a city where the garbage trucks stop functioning – the accumulation of waste eventually becomes overwhelming, disrupting the city's normal operations.

Beyond these individual components, the cell's internal organization is a marvel of engineering. The cytoskeleton, a network of protein filaments, provides structural support and facilitates intracellular transport. Imagine this as the city's infrastructure – roads, bridges, and communication lines. Disruptions to the cytoskeleton can lead to cellular dysfunction, highlighting the importance of maintaining structural integrity.

But the cellular world isn't just about internal processes; it's also about interactions with the external environment. Cell membranes, acting as gatekeepers, control the passage of substances into and out of the cell. These membranes are incredibly selective, allowing only certain molecules to pass through. Disruptions to membrane integrity, caused by toxins or pathogens, can have devastating consequences. It's like a city's borders being breached, allowing unwanted intruders to wreak havoc.

The process of cell division, where a single cell divides into two daughter cells, is another remarkable feat of cellular engineering. This process, known as mitosis, is meticulously controlled to ensure accurate chromosome segregation. Errors during mitosis, however, can lead to aneuploidy, a condition where cells have an abnormal number of chromosomes. This can cause various genetic disorders and even contribute to cancer development. It's like a city's population census going horribly wrong, leading to societal imbalances and potential instability.

And let's not forget the amazing ability of cells to repair themselves. DNA damage, caused by various factors such as radiation or chemicals, is constantly occurring. Cells possess sophisticated mechanisms to repair this damage, ensuring the integrity of the genome. However, these repair mechanisms are not always perfect. Errors in DNA repair can lead to mutations, some of which can be harmful, while others may contribute to evolution. It's like the city's repair crews working tirelessly to fix damage, but occasionally making mistakes that have unforeseen consequences.

The study of cells and their functions is not only scientifically fascinating but also holds immense medical significance. Understanding the intricacies of cellular processes is essential for developing treatments for various diseases, from cancer to genetic disorders. The more we learn about the remarkable capabilities and occasional mishaps of cells, the better equipped we are to address health challenges and improve human well-being. Consider the intricate dance of cellular processes – a symphony of molecular interactions that, when harmonious, creates the miracle of life, and when disrupted, leads to the complexities of disease.

The astonishing precision of cellular mechanisms is often overshadowed by the sheer volume of actions happening simultaneously. Think of the countless chemical reactions, the coordinated movements of molecules, the intricate signalling pathways – it's a level of organization that dwarfs even the most complex human-designed systems. Yet, within this intricate system, errors do occur, and these errors, often subtle and initially insignificant, can have cascading effects, leading to cellular dysfunction and disease.

For instance, the process of protein folding, crucial for the proper functioning of countless cellular proteins, is a delicate and intricate process. Errors in protein folding can lead to the accumulation of misfolded proteins, which can trigger various diseases, including Alzheimer's disease and Parkinson's disease. These misfolded proteins are like faulty parts in a complex machine, disrupting the smooth functioning of the entire system.

Similarly, the regulation of gene expression, the process by which genes are turned on or off, is another finely tuned process essential for cellular function. Errors in gene regulation can lead to an overproduction or underproduction of vital proteins, resulting in various diseases. It's like a city's resource allocation system malfunctioning – some areas receive too much, while others are starved of resources.

The study of cellular biology is continually revealing new layers of complexity and sophistication. Advanced imaging techniques, such as electron microscopy and advanced fluorescence microscopy, allow scientists to visualize cellular structures and processes in unprecedented detail. These technologies provide invaluable insights into the inner workings of cells, revealing the beauty and complexity of the cellular world. It is akin to having a high-resolution map of the city, allowing us to appreciate its intricate infrastructure and pinpoint the sources of dysfunction.

Furthermore, advancements in genomics and proteomics allow scientists to study the entire genome and proteome of cells, providing comprehensive information on the genes and proteins that make up cells. This "big data" approach provides a more holistic understanding of cellular function and dysfunction, moving beyond individual components to the interconnectedness of the entire system. This is like having access to a complete database of the city's population, industries, and infrastructure, providing a panoramic view of its organization and operations.

The field of cellular biology is a rapidly evolving one, constantly pushing the boundaries of our understanding. New discoveries are continuously being made, uncovering new layers of complexity and refining our understanding of cellular processes. It is a testament to the ongoing scientific quest to unravel the mysteries of life, to comprehend the elegance and efficiency of the cellular world. It's like exploring a vast and uncharted territory, with new discoveries constantly revealing the extent and complexity of this microscopic universe.

The surprising world of cells is a testament to the power of natural selection, the relentless process that has shaped life on Earth. The cellular mechanisms that we observe today are the result of billions of years of evolution, refinement, and adaptation. Each cell, in its own way, is a marvel of engineering, a testament to the power of evolution to create complex and efficient systems. It's a city that has evolved over millennia, constantly adapting to challenges and improving its efficiency. The story of cells is a story of adaptation, resilience, and the persistent struggle for survival.

The study of cellular blunders, therefore, provides crucial insights into the mechanisms of disease and the importance of maintaining cellular health. By understanding how and why cells malfunction, we can develop more effective treatments for a wide range of diseases. The exploration of the cellular world is an ongoing journey, with each new discovery deepening our understanding of life's intricate processes. It's a journey of exploration, discovery, and continuous learning, driven by an unquenchable curiosity about the wonders of life at the microscopic level. The cellular world, despite its occasional blunders, remains a testament to the breathtaking elegance and efficiency of life itself.

Ancient Empires & Forgotten Civilizations

FORGET the pyramids and the Roman Empire for a moment; we're diving into the fascinating, often-overlooked world of ancient civilizations that deserve a much bigger spotlight. While the empires of Egypt and Rome loom large in our collective historical imagination, countless other societies flourished and left behind legacies as impressive, if less widely known. This isn't just about dusty artefacts and crumbling ruins; these civilizations offer unique insights into human ingenuity, resilience, and the sheer diversity of human experience across millennia.

Let's start with the Nabataeans, a remarkably resourceful people who carved out a thriving civilization in the arid landscapes of present-day Jordan and parts of Syria and Saudi Arabia. Flourishing from around the 6th century BCE to the 1st century CE, their ingenuity in water management is particularly noteworthy. In a region perpetually challenged by water scarcity, they developed an intricate system of cisterns, dams, and canals that allowed them to cultivate the land, create lush oases, and support a significant population in what would seem an impossibly harsh environment. Their capital, Petra, carved into sandstone cliffs, stands as a testament to their architectural prowess and mastery of engineering. Petra, with its stunning rock-cut architecture and intricate network of water channels, isn't just a beautiful sight; it's a compelling demonstration of how human ingenuity can overcome even the most formidable environmental obstacles. The Nabataeans' trading acumen also played a key role in their success. Positioned along crucial trade routes between the East and the West, they expertly facilitated the movement of goods, further contributing to their economic prosperity and cultural exchange. Their sophisticated system of water management wasn't just a technological marvel; it was the foundation upon which a whole culture flourished.

Next, we journey to the Indus Valley Civilization, one of the world's oldest urban societies, which thrived in present-day India and Pakistan around 3300 to 1300 BCE. This civilization, pre-dating even the ancient Egyptians, boasts an impressive level of urban planning, with cities like Mohenjo-daro and Harappa featuring sophisticated grid patterns, drainage systems, and standardized weights and measures. These weren't just haphazard settlements; they were carefully planned urban centres that reveal a remarkable level of societal organization and engineering expertise. While much remains mysterious about the Indus Valley Civilization, including their writing system, which remains undeciphered, the sheer scale and complexity of their urban planning is a profound testament to their advanced technological abilities. Archaeological discoveries continue to unveil new facets of this civilization, steadily expanding our understanding of their daily lives, social structures, and overall significance in human history. Their advanced urban planning suggests a level of centralized governance and social organization that was incredibly advanced for its time. The standardized bricks and grid-like street plans suggest a level of engineering expertise that foreshadows much later advancements.

Moving further east, we encounter the mysterious civilization of Angkor, in present-day Cambodia. From the 9th to the 15th centuries CE, the Khmer Empire built magnificent temples and cities, the most renowned being Angkor Wat, a breathtaking architectural masterpiece. The scale and artistry of Angkor Wat, with its intricate carvings and massive stone structures, speak volumes about the Khmer Empire's power, wealth, and religious devotion. The sheer size and intricacy of the structures, combined with the sophisticated hydraulic systems used to manage the surrounding water resources, illustrate the Empire's advanced technological capabilities and resource management strategies. Angkor wasn't just a single temple; it was a sprawling complex of temples, palaces, and reservoirs, demonstrating a level of urban planning and architectural sophistication unmatched in Southeast Asia at the time. What makes Angkor even more fascinating is the ongoing mystery surrounding the reasons for the decline and abandonment of this magnificent city. Theories range from ecological catastrophes to societal upheaval, highlighting the complex interplay of factors that can shape even the mightiest of empires.

Now, let's delve into the less-known, but equally fascinating, world of the Puebloans of the American Southwest. These people, known for their cliff dwellings and intricate irrigation systems, created thriving communities in what is now Arizona, New Mexico, Colorado, and Utah. Their cliff dwellings, perched precariously on the sides of canyons, weren't just homes; they were carefully designed settlements providing defensive positions and access to water and resources. Their mastery of irrigation in a harsh environment provided the foundation for their agricultural success and allowed them to sustain relatively large populations. The construction of these cliff dwellings required incredible ingenuity, highlighting their expertise in engineering and problem-solving. The Puebloans' advanced knowledge of astronomy and their sophisticated understanding of their environment demonstrate their remarkable adaptation to the challenges of the desert landscape. The intricate designs of their pottery and the durability of their architecture speak to their refined skills and the lasting impact of their culture. Their resilience in the face of environmental challenges and their innovative approach to community building continues to inspire awe and admiration.

But the story of forgotten civilizations doesn't end there. Consider the Olmec civilization of ancient Mexico, known for their colossal basalt heads and sophisticated social structures. Their influence on later Mesoamerican cultures is undeniable, yet the intricacies of their own society still hold many mysteries. The colossal basalt heads, transported over vast distances, are a stark reminder of their impressive organizational skills and engineering capabilities. Their intricate carvings and the development of a complex writing system highlight their advanced artistic and intellectual achievements. The Olmec's influence extended far beyond their immediate geographical area, with evidence suggesting cultural exchange and interactions with other groups, underscoring their significant role in the cultural landscape of ancient Mexico.

These are just a few examples of the numerous fascinating and often overlooked ancient civilizations. From the ingenious water management of the Nabataeans to the advanced urban planning of the Indus Valley Civilization and the breathtaking architecture of Angkor and the ingenuity of the Puebloans, the world is rich with stories of remarkable human achievement. These civilizations offer valuable lessons about the resilience, creativity, and ingenuity of our ancestors and inspire us to look beyond the well-trodden paths of history to discover the hidden gems of human experience. Each civilization boasts its unique character, culture, and historical significance, each contributing in its own unique way to the rich tapestry of human history. Their stories remind us that history is far more diverse and complex than the narratives often presented in textbooks, and that the past holds countless more secrets waiting to be unearthed. The more we learn about these forgotten civilizations, the more we understand the astonishing depth and breadth of human civilization throughout history.

Myths & Realities
of the Middle Ages

THE Middle Ages: a period often caricatured as a time of darkness and superstition, a monotonous stretch of time between the glories of Rome and the Renaissance. But peel back the layers of dusty textbooks and romanticized notions, and you'll discover a vibrant, surprisingly advanced era brimming with innovation, artistic flourishing, and yes, even a healthy dose of the bizarre. Forget the simplistic narrative; medieval history is far more nuanced and captivating than you might think. Let's dive into some unexpected realities, shattering a few myths along the way.

One persistent myth is the image of medieval people as perpetually filthy, wallowing in disease and grime. While hygiene standards certainly weren't on par with our modern expectations, the reality was more complex. The notion of a "Great Stink" pervading medieval cities is a gross oversimplification. Bathhouses, though perhaps not as numerous as in Roman times, still existed in many parts of Europe, particularly in the larger cities. Cleanliness, however, was more about social status than universal practice. The wealthy had access to baths and fresh linens, while the poor had to make do with limited resources. Personal hygiene was certainly influenced by religious beliefs; the emphasis on ritual purification meant frequent washing for those who could afford it. The concept of "cleanliness" itself also differed significantly. The lack of germ theory meant that cleanliness was more about outward appearance and the avoidance of visible dirt rather than a concern about microscopic pathogens.

Another misconception is the supposed intellectual stagnation of the Middle Ages. The "Dark Ages" label is thoroughly misleading. This era saw the flourishing of universities, the preservation and translation of classical texts, and significant advancements in various fields of knowledge. Think about the architectural marvels of the Gothic cathedrals – breathtaking feats of engineering and artistic expression that defied the capabilities of their time. These magnificent structures weren't just religious edifices; they were symbols of ingenuity and scientific understanding, pushing the boundaries of architecture and engineering. Their construction required complex calculations, sophisticated scaffolding systems, and a deep understanding of mechanics. It's easy to overlook the intellectual and scientific progress embedded within these stunning feats. The development of new technologies, for example the pointed arch which provided a greater stability and allowed for higher structures, is a testament to the innovation of the time.

Furthermore, medieval medicine, often portrayed as primitive and barbaric, demonstrated surprising sophistication in certain areas. While bloodletting and other questionable practices existed, medieval physicians also made valuable contributions to medical knowledge, translating and commenting on classical texts, and developing new medical treatises and practices. The study of herbs and their medicinal properties, for instance, was relatively advanced, with sophisticated herbal pharmacopoeias outlining the uses and properties of various plants. The creation of hospitals and the development of surgical techniques, though rudimentary by modern standards, represent notable steps forward in medical care. It's important to remember that medical knowledge was limited by the lack of understanding of microbiology, but to call their work entirely ineffective is an unfair and inaccurate portrayal.

The military technology of the Middle Ages also deserves a closer examination. The simplistic view often paints medieval warfare as a chaotic melee of swords and shields. The reality was significantly more sophisticated. The development and refinement of siege weaponry, such as catapults and trebuchets, represent remarkable feats of mechanical engineering. These were not crude devices; they were products of careful design and calculation, capable of delivering devastating blows to enemy fortifications. Similarly, the evolution of armour and weaponry, from chainmail to plate armour, showcases a constant drive for technological improvement, reflecting a deep understanding of both metallurgy and battlefield dynamics. Think about the intricate design and engineering involved in constructing a suit of plate armour; it's a masterpiece of protection that highlights the metalworking skills of the era. This technological advancement was vital for military success, and its impact significantly shaped the political landscape of the time.

The arts and literature of the Middle Ages were remarkably diverse and rich. The common misconception of a monolithic culture is far from accurate. From the grandeur of Romanesque architecture to the soaring heights of Gothic cathedrals, the artistic achievements of the period are undeniable. Manuscripts, painstakingly illuminated with exquisite detail, showcase artistic skill and cultural importance. These were not mere books; they were treasured artefacts, preserving knowledge and beauty for future generations. Likewise, medieval literature, though largely written in Latin, ranged from religious texts and epic poems to courtly romances and fabliaux, demonstrating a diversity of styles and themes that continues to resonate today. The stories and poems of the era offer compelling insights into the beliefs, values and social norms of the time.

Furthermore, the common perception of a rigid, monolithic social structure in the Middle Ages needs reconsideration. While feudalism played a significant role, social mobility existed to a degree often overlooked. The reality is that society was far more fluid than often depicted, with people moving up and down the social ladder, albeit often slowly and gradually. Merchants and craftsmen gained wealth and influence, sometimes achieving remarkable social standing. Social status and mobility was complex, dependent on factors such as wealth, family connections, land ownership and individual skills. The rigid hierarchical structure was only a part of a more dynamic and complex reality.

Finally, let's address the pervasive myth of universal religious uniformity. The Middle Ages were not a period of blind faith and unquestioning obedience to the Church. Heresy, dissent, and religious conflicts were far from uncommon. The Cathar movement, for example, presented a significant challenge to the authority of the Catholic Church, leading to violent conflict and persecution. Similarly, various reform movements within the Church itself indicate a diverse range of beliefs and practices. Religious uniformity was an ideal, rather than an achieved reality, and it's important to remember the diversity of religious expression in this era. This diversity sometimes led to conflict and persecution, but it is nonetheless significant in highlighting the complex dynamics and tensions within society.

In conclusion, the Middle Ages, far from being a monolithic period of darkness and stagnation, were a dynamic and complex era with surprising advancements, creative flourishes, and often-overlooked complexities. By challenging common misconceptions and appreciating the rich tapestry of medieval life, we gain a far more nuanced and accurate understanding of this pivotal period in human history. The medieval world, with all its complexities, contradictions, and fascinating realities, invites further exploration. Its history is far more vibrant and interesting than the simplistic narratives often presented. The more we delve into its details, the more remarkable this often-misunderstood era becomes. The myths surrounding it only serve to obscure its true depth and richness.

Unexpected Turns in History

THE fall of Constantinople in 1453, often cited as a pivotal moment marking the end of the Byzantine Empire and the beginning of the Ottoman dominance, wasn't the clean, decisive victory history books often portray. While the Ottoman conquest is undeniably a landmark event, the reality is far messier, more nuanced, and surprisingly less inevitable than commonly understood. The city's defences, long considered impregnable, were weakened by internal strife, political manoeuvring, and a chronic lack of sufficient manpower to withstand a sustained siege. The Emperor Constantine XI, despite his valiant efforts, faced a desperate situation exacerbated by a lack of substantial Western support, despite the looming threat to Christendom. The fall itself was a brutal culmination of years of escalating tension and strategic miscalculations, painting a complex picture beyond a simple narrative of conquest. The prolonged siege, punctuated by moments of both fierce resistance and desperate hope, ultimately highlighted the vulnerability of even the most formidable empires in the face of relentless pressure and internal weaknesses.

The American Revolution, often romanticized as a heroic struggle against tyrannical rule, presents several unexpected twists when examined closely. While the colonists' desire for liberty and self-governance is undeniable, the revolutionary cause was far from unified. Loyalists, who remained steadfast in their allegiance to the British crown, comprised a significant portion of the colonial population. Their motivations were varied – some held genuine loyalty to the monarchy, others feared the consequences of rebellion, and some simply benefited from the existing system. This internal division significantly hampered the revolutionary effort, forcing the patriots to navigate complex political landscapes and contend with internal opposition alongside external threats.

The financial factors involved where predominately due to the 'Tea Tax' which the British enforced. However, some colonials 'acquired' there own tea and sold this at a cheaper price than the British taxed tea which was coming in through the ports. When the British tea was not being sold the tax was lifted by the Crown. This then meant that the British un-taxed tea was now cheaper than the tea sold by local entrepreneurs; The Boston Tea Party may have been a statement to the Crown, or as other historians tend to believe it was just a show of strength by local businessmen to protect their profits.

The war's outcome, seemingly predetermined by the colonists' ultimate victory, was far from certain throughout its protracted course. The British, initially confident in their superior military might, faced unexpected challenges in navigating the unfamiliar terrain and confronting the determined resistance of the colonial militias. The pivotal role played by foreign powers, notably France, further underscores the intricate interplay of international relations that ultimately shaped the revolution's trajectory. The eventual victory, therefore, wasn't a foregone conclusion but rather a result of a complex confluence of factors, including military strategy, diplomatic manoeuvring, and a persistent, albeit fractured, revolutionary spirit.

The invention of the printing press, commonly credited to Johannes Gutenberg around 1440, isn't a straightforward tale of singular genius. While Gutenberg's contribution was undeniably significant, his invention was the culmination of decades, perhaps even centuries, of incremental advancements in printing technology. Woodblock printing, for instance, had been widely practiced in East Asia for centuries, paving the way for more sophisticated techniques. Moreover, Gutenberg himself was embroiled in legal battles and financial difficulties, highlighting the challenges of translating a ground-breaking invention into a profitable enterprise. The widespread adoption of the printing press wasn't instantaneous; its impact unfolded gradually, initially affecting a limited segment of society. The accessibility of information, though transformative, was a slow burn, dependent on factors like literacy rates, cost of production, and the evolving political and social landscapes. The revolutionary power of the printing press wasn't inherent in the technology itself, but rather in its eventual integration into societal structures and its capacity to disseminate ideas across geographical and social boundaries.

The Industrial Revolution, a period of unprecedented technological advancement, also unfolded in a manner far more intricate than commonly perceived. While the technological innovations are undeniable – the steam engine, the power loom, the cotton gin – the transformation wasn't uniform across all sectors of society. The benefits of industrialization weren't evenly distributed, resulting in vast disparities in wealth and creating new social classes. The rise of factories also led to appalling working conditions, including child labour and long hours in dangerous environments, starkly contrasting with the image of progress frequently associated with this era. The impact on the environment was equally significant and largely negative, with industrial pollution contributing to widespread environmental degradation. The narrative of unfettered progress thus needs to be tempered by a realistic assessment of the social and environmental costs of industrialization, revealing a complex legacy that continues to shape our world today. The revolution wasn't simply a linear progression; it was a chaotic process marked by periods of rapid growth interspersed with economic downturns, social unrest, and significant human suffering.

The discovery of penicillin, often presented as a serendipitous moment of scientific brilliance, showcases the often-overlooked role of chance encounters and collaborative efforts in scientific breakthroughs. Alexander Fleming's observation of mould inhibiting bacterial growth was certainly pivotal, but the path from that observation to the mass production of penicillin was far from straightforward. Years of research, refinement, and collaboration were necessary to isolate and purify the active compound, overcome challenges in scaling up production, and develop effective methods of administration. The wartime urgency accelerated the process, underscoring the impact of external pressures on scientific advancement. The story of penicillin, therefore, is not merely one of individual genius but also of collective effort, painstaking research, and the convergence of several crucial factors that ultimately transformed the treatment of bacterial infections. The miraculous drug was the result of a long and complex journey, not simply a 'eureka' moment.

The Cold War, often framed as a bipolar struggle between the United States and the Soviet Union, encompassed a multitude of complexities and unexpected alliances that defy simplistic narratives. While the ideological conflict between capitalism and communism was central to the Cold War, it was played out through a complex web of proxy wars, covert operations, and shifting geopolitical alignments. The involvement of numerous countries, each with its own national interests and internal struggles, added layers of complexity to the geopolitical landscape. Moreover, the constant threat of nuclear annihilation cast a long shadow, shaping international relations and domestic policies in profound ways. The Cold War's outcome, far from being a predictable clash of titans, was significantly influenced by factors like economic competition, technological advancements, and the shifting internal dynamics within both superpowers. The eventual collapse of the Soviet Union wasn't a foregone conclusion but rather a dramatic culmination of sustained internal pressures and external factors, revealing a far more nuanced picture than a simple narrative of superpower conflict.

The space race, frequently portrayed as a straightforward competition between the US and the USSR, reveals fascinating complexities when delved into further. While the competition between the two superpowers provided a powerful impetus for technological advancement, the race was also propelled by a multitude of factors, including national pride, ideological posturing, and the pursuit of scientific knowledge. The technological leaps made during this era – from rocketry to telecommunications – were transformative, extending far beyond the immediate goal of reaching space. However, the space race also highlighted the enormous costs, both financial and human, associated with such ambitious endeavours. Moreover, the narrative often overlooks the contributions of countless scientists, engineers, and technicians from diverse backgrounds whose collective efforts made these monumental achievements possible. The space race, therefore, was far more than a simple contest; it was a complex undertaking with far-reaching consequences that continue to resonate today, a testament to human ingenuity and ambition, but also to the considerable challenges and ethical considerations involved.

These examples, though far from exhaustive, demonstrate a recurring theme: History, when viewed through a detailed lens, reveals a multitude of surprising turns, unexpected outcomes, and complex interplays of factors that often defy simplistic narratives. The simplistic, often-repeated narratives of historical events mask the rich complexity and often contradictory nature of the past. Digging beneath the surface reveals a far more nuanced and engrossing story, richer and more informative than simple summaries would suggest. The pursuit of a more complete and accurate understanding of the past requires a willingness to challenge assumptions, explore complexities, and appreciate the unexpected turns that shape the course of human history. It is through this kind of deep exploration that we can truly gain a richer and more meaningful understanding of our world and our place within it. The stories of the past are not simply linear accounts but intricate tapestries woven with threads of chance, ambition, human fallibility, and unexpected consequences. These complexities enrich our understanding and make the study of history so incredibly engaging.

The Curious Case of Lost Cities

THE echoes of vanished civilizations whisper through the ages, leaving behind tantalizing fragments of their existence. Lost cities, swallowed by jungles, buried beneath sands, or submerged beneath the waves, continue to capture our imaginations, sparking debates and fuelling expeditions. These aren't just geographical anomalies; they represent lost chapters in the grand narrative of human history, each disappearance a puzzle box waiting to be unlocked.

Take, for example, the enigmatic city of El Dorado, a name synonymous with untold riches and a shimmering city of gold. While the literal "city of gold" likely exists only in legend, the myth itself reflects a deeper historical truth: the allure of lost civilizations and the persistent human fascination with uncovering their secrets. Spanish conquistadors, driven by greed and glory, spent centuries searching for El Dorado, their quests often leading them to real, albeit less glamorous, pre-Columbian settlements in the Amazon basin and the Andes mountains. Their frantic searches, while ultimately unsuccessful in finding the legendary golden city, inadvertently unearthed a wealth of information about the sophisticated cultures that thrived in the region long before European arrival. The very hunt for El Dorado, therefore, inadvertently fuelled significant archaeological discoveries, demonstrating how myth and reality often intertwine in the exploration of lost cities.

The legendary city of Atlantis, perpetually shrouded in mystery, offers a different kind of enigma. Plato's account, woven into his philosophical dialogues, portrays a technologically advanced island civilization that vanished beneath the waves. While no conclusive evidence supports the existence of Atlantis as described by Plato, the myth persists, fuelling countless books, films, and even pseudo-scientific theories. However, the enduring power of the Atlantis myth underscores our deep-seated curiosity about advanced societies that might have preceded or existed alongside our own. The relentless search for Atlantis, whether successful or not, has inspired generations of researchers to explore underwater archaeology and delve deeper into the mysteries of our planet's submerged past. This serves as a poignant example of how a myth, however fantastical, can drive real-world exploration and contribute to our knowledge of history and geography.

Moving from the realm of myth to the realm of documented history, we encounter the fascinating case of Petra, the "Rose City" of Jordan. Carved into sandstone cliffs, Petra was a bustling Nabataean metropolis, a crossroads of trade routes in the ancient world. Its intricate rock-cut architecture, water management systems, and elaborate tombs stand as testaments to the Nabataeans' ingenuity and architectural prowess. While Petra wasn't exactly "lost" in the sense of being entirely forgotten, it was largely abandoned and largely unknown to the outside world for centuries after its decline. Its rediscovery in the early 19th century reintroduced the world to this extraordinary city, providing invaluable insights into a previously obscure culture. The gradual uncovering of Petra highlights the vital role of serendipitous discovery in unearthing the past and the ongoing process of historical reconstruction. It's a reminder that even well-documented histories can hold previously hidden layers awaiting careful examination.

Another fascinating case is that of Angkor, a vast complex of temples and palaces in Cambodia. For centuries, this magnificent city lay hidden beneath the jungle, its grandeur gradually reclaimed by the encroaching rainforest. The gradual rediscovery of Angkor, spanning several centuries, revealed a complex civilization, the Khmer Empire, that thrived for over six centuries. The scale of Angkor, with its monumental temples like Angkor Wat, speaks to the immense power and sophisticated artistry of the Khmer people. The reclamation of Angkor from the jungle showcases the power of nature to both conceal and preserve historical wonders, a cyclical process demonstrating the enduring resilience of both civilization and the environment. The ongoing archaeological work at Angkor continues to provide new insights into Khmer culture, demonstrating how the study of lost cities is an ongoing process of discovery and interpretation.

The stories of these lost cities, while vastly different in their specifics, share common threads. They each highlight the impermanence of human civilizations and the unpredictable forces—both natural and human—that can lead to their decline and disappearance. Moreover, the persistent human desire to uncover these lost worlds fuels ongoing exploration, archaeological investigation, and our deeper understanding of the past. The processes of rediscovery and reinterpretation are dynamic and ongoing, reflecting the evolution of our own knowledge and technological capabilities.

Furthermore, the study of lost cities is not simply about unearthing physical remains; it's about reconstructing narratives, piecing together fragments of information to create a more complete picture of past societies. Each lost city represents a unique cultural expression, a window into different social structures, beliefs, and technologies. The painstaking work of archaeologists, historians, and other scholars helps us understand not only the physical structures of these lost cities but also the complexities of the human societies that built and inhabited them. We learn about their economic systems, religious practices, social hierarchies, and daily lives – creating a three-dimensional portrait far richer than any simple narrative of rise and fall.

The process of piecing together these narratives often involves interpreting ambiguous evidence. Archaeological finds can be fragmented, and written records, if they exist at all, are often incomplete or biased. This presents significant challenges to researchers, forcing them to use deductive reasoning and creative interpretation to construct plausible accounts of these vanished civilizations. The resulting narratives are not definitive truths, but rather, the best current interpretations based on available evidence. This inherently provisional nature of historical understanding adds to the intrigue, emphasizing that the study of lost cities is a continually evolving process.

Consider the ongoing debate surrounding the collapse of the Maya civilization. While environmental factors, such as drought, played a significant role, internal strife, overpopulation, and unsustainable resource management likely contributed as well. The unravelling of the Maya's sophisticated societal structure wasn't a single cataclysmic event, but rather, a gradual process of decline and transformation spread across centuries. The rediscovery and ongoing study of Mayan cities reveal the intricate social and political dynamics that existed within this civilization. It showcases that the fall of a great civilization is seldom a simple narrative but rather a complex interplay of environmental and societal factors that are still being debated today.

The search for lost cities is more than just an academic pursuit; it's a reflection of our own human curiosity and our enduring fascination with our past. These vanished worlds offer a sense of wonder, a chance to connect with previous generations, and a reminder of the resilience and ingenuity of humanity throughout history. They also act as cautionary tales, highlighting the fragility of civilizations and the importance of sustainable practices. The quest for these lost cities is an ongoing journey of discovery, filled with mystery, intrigue, and an unending pursuit of knowledge about ourselves and the world we inhabit. Each newly unearthed artefact, each deciphered inscription, each architectural feature uncovered, contributes to a richer understanding of the past, reminding us that the stories of lost cities are far from over. Their narratives continue to unfold, one discovery at a time.

Unexpected Anecdotes from Conflicts

THE transition from the hushed whispers of lost civilizations to the thunderous roar of global conflict might seem jarring, but the human impulse to explore the unknown, to puzzle over the inexplicable, remains constant. World War I and II, cataclysmic events that reshaped the geopolitical landscape, also yielded a bizarre harvest of unexpected anecdotes, tales so strange they often seem plucked from fiction rather than the grim reality of global war. Let's delve into some of these unexpected twists, turning points that demonstrate just how unpredictable the course of history can truly be.

For instance, consider the role of animals in the conflict. While the image of warhorses charging into battle is relatively familiar, the contribution of other animals is far less well-documented. Consider the pigeons, for instance, not just any pigeons, but specially trained birds whose remarkable navigational skills proved vital for delivering crucial messages across the ravaged battlefields. These feathered heroes braved enemy fire, treacherous weather, and the perils of being hunted, their tiny bodies carrying the weight of vital information, sometimes even tipping the scales of critical battles. Their bravery deserves far more recognition than they've received. Some even earned medals! While we celebrate the bravery of human soldiers, the unwavering dedication of these avian messengers should not be overlooked. Their stories are a testament to the unexpected alliances forged in the crucible of war, a surprisingly poignant detail often overlooked in the grand narrative of these conflicts.

Then there's the story of the "ghost army," a unit of the US Army tasked with a particularly ingenious deception operation. This group of skilled actors, artists, and engineers created incredibly realistic-sounding tank divisions and artillery batteries using inflatable tanks, sound effects, and clever radio jamming. They effectively "painted" a phantom army onto the map, successfully diverting German troops and resources away from genuine allied operations. Their mission was a masterpiece of psychological warfare, proving that even illusion can play a decisive role in armed conflict. Their successes are a testament to ingenuity, proving that sometimes, a clever trick is more effective than brute force. This little-known unit deserves a place in the annals of unconventional warfare.

The impact of weather, often underestimated, played a surprisingly decisive role in both World Wars. The infamous "Great Blizzard" of 1917 during World War I, for example, crippled German offensive operations on the Eastern Front, effectively delaying the offensive and giving the opposing forces a chance to regroup. The freezing conditions caused havoc with military equipment, leading to logistical nightmares and effectively freezing the conflict in its tracks for a significant period. Nature, it seems, has an uncanny habit of intervening in the most unexpected ways, sometimes tipping the balance of war.

World War II saw the remarkable use of code-breaking as a crucial turning point. At Bletchley Park, a team of mathematicians and cryptographers worked tirelessly to decipher the German Enigma code. Their work, famously characterized by the use of early computers, provided Allied forces with vital intelligence, shortening the war and potentially saving countless lives. The story of Bletchley Park shows us how the power of intelligence, even in its most abstract forms, can be as potent a weapon as any tank or battleship. They were truly unsung heroes, their contributions as essential as those on the front lines.

Beyond official military strategies, individual acts of ingenuity and resilience also played a significant role. Stories abound of civilian populations displaying remarkable resourcefulness, adapting to wartime conditions with a creativity that bordered on the miraculous. Consider the innovative ways communities repurposed resources, adapting their diets to accommodate food shortages, finding creative solutions to everyday problems under the ever-present threat of bombing raids. These often-overlooked aspects of wartime life reveal the human spirit's resilience, its ability to adapt, and to find hope even in the darkest of times. Their stories are a vital part of the wartime narrative, a reminder of the human capacity to overcome adversity.

In the realm of espionage, numerous unbelievable stories emerged. Double agents, clandestine operations, and daring escapes filled the pages of wartime history, some of these events stranger than fiction. The feats of ingenuity, deception, and sheer bravery displayed by spies on both sides remain captivating. The stories are shrouded in secrecy, making them more intriguing, tales of courage, betrayal, and unwavering dedication in the face of mortal danger. The world of espionage during wartime holds a particular fascination because of its inherent unpredictability and the often-blurred lines between reality and fiction.

Consider the case of the "Operation Mincemeat," a British deception plan during World War II that involved planting a body of a dead man with fake documents on the coast of Spain. The ruse, incredibly audacious, successfully misled the Axis powers into believing the Allied invasion of Sicily was directed elsewhere. Operation Mincemeat is a stunning example of how audacious plans, meticulously crafted and perfectly executed, can reshape the course of war. Its audaciousness is a testament to how creativity and bold thinking can turn the tides of conflict.

Even the seemingly mundane aspects of wartime life yielded surprising anecdotes. The challenges of maintaining morale among troops, the ingenuity of field kitchens, the evolution of military slang – each element contributed to the unique character of the war experience. These seemingly minor details, though often overlooked, offer valuable glimpses into the daily lives of soldiers and civilians alike. The hardships faced, the resilience shown, the unexpected forms of camaraderie developed — all reveal a depth and complexity often missing from grand narratives.

The unexpected innovations spurred by necessity also deserve mention. From the development of penicillin to the advancements in radar technology, World War II, despite its horrors, fostered extraordinary leaps in scientific and technological fields. These breakthroughs had a lasting impact on society, demonstrating how even in the face of destruction, humanity's capacity for innovation remains remarkable. The world was irrevocably changed not only by bombs and bullets but by a surge of technological and scientific progress. These advances weren't mere by-products; they were integral to the conflict itself, altering its trajectory in profound ways.

Finally, remember the lasting legacies of these conflicts. The Treaty of Versailles, for example, a consequence of World War I, was a flawed attempt at peace that contributed to the rise of tensions that eventually led to World War II. This highlights how even the attempts to resolve conflict can have unforeseen and often damaging consequences. The agreements forged after conflict often shape future relations, sometimes in unpredictable ways, underscoring the long-term impact of these events.

The stories of World War I and II are filled with surprising twists, heroic acts, and unbelievable events. These anecdotes, often relegated to footnotes in history books, bring these conflicts to life in ways that dry statistical analysis never could. They remind us that the human element—with its mixture of heroism, folly, courage, and sheer absurdity—is often the most compelling part of any historical narrative, particularly one as momentous as these two world wars. They are a testament to the unpredictability of human nature, the enduring power of human ingenuity, and the remarkable capacity for both destruction and creation that exists within the human spirit. The narratives of these conflicts continue to resonate, not just because of their scale, but because of the unexpected human stories interwoven within them.

Exploring Remote Islands

FORGET your usual vacation hotspots; we're diving into the extraordinary realm of remote islands, places so unique they seem plucked from a fantasy novel. These aren't your typical tourist traps; we're talking about islands that defy expectations, harbouring secrets both geological and cultural. Prepare for a voyage into the wildly diverse and often bizarre landscapes that dot our oceans.

Let's start with Socotra, an archipelago off the coast of Yemen. This island feels like it belongs on another planet entirely. Its alien flora – the dragon's blood tree, with its otherworldly, umbrella-shaped crown, is a prime example – has evolved in such isolation that a significant percentage of its plant life is found nowhere else on Earth. Imagine landscapes painted in shades of jade and crimson, sculpted by millennia of wind and sun. The isolation has also nurtured a unique culture, a blend of ancient traditions and modern influences. The Socotran language, for instance, is a fascinating linguistic outlier, showcasing the island's distinct cultural heritage. But this breathtaking beauty is vulnerable. The impact of climate change and development is a growing concern, threatening this extraordinary ecosystem. Socotra serves as a potent reminder of the delicate balance between human progress and the preservation of our planet's irreplaceable treasures.

Next, consider the volcanic wonders of the Galapagos Islands. Made famous by Charles Darwin's observations, these islands are a living laboratory of evolution. Giant tortoises lumber across lava fields, blue-footed boobies perform elaborate mating dances, and marine iguanas graze on algae – a spectacle unique to this archipelago. The very geology of the islands, formed by volcanic activity, has dictated the evolution of its unique species, leading to a fascinating display of adaptation. This isolated ecosystem, while captivating, has proven vulnerable. Human encroachment, the introduction of invasive species, and the ever-present threat of climate change continually challenge the delicate balance of this natural marvel. The Galapagos' story is a compelling blend of scientific wonder and a stark reminder of humanity's impact on the natural world.

Now, let's journey to Easter Island (Rapa Nui), a tiny speck of land in the vast expanse of the Pacific Ocean. Famous for its iconic moai statues, the island offers a poignant reflection on human ingenuity and the consequences of unsustainable practices. The sheer scale of the stone carving, the mystery surrounding their construction, and the eventual societal collapse of the island's inhabitants are a compelling story of human endeavour and ecological fragility. This remote outpost stands as a potent symbol of our past and a cautionary tale for the future.

The remote, uninhabited islands of Tristan da Cunha, a volcanic archipelago in the south Atlantic, offer a starkly different perspective. Imagine an ecosystem untouched by human development, a place where the only sounds are the wind and the waves. Tristan da Cunha represents the raw, untamed beauty of the natural world, a sanctuary where wildlife thrives in an almost pristine environment. However, even here, the reach of human impact is felt, with the threat of pollution and climate change reaching even these remote shores. The pristine beauty of Tristan da Cunha emphasizes the importance of global efforts to protect even the most secluded corners of our planet.

The Faroe Islands, a collection of rugged volcanic islands in the North Atlantic, offer a different kind of remoteness. Here, the human element is integral to the landscape. Steep cliffs, dramatic waterfalls, and charming villages clinging to the coastline create a landscape both breathtaking and deeply human. The culture of the Faroe Islands, with its rich maritime heritage and strong community bonds, is intimately intertwined with its dramatic surroundings. The islanders' way of life offers a fascinating glimpse into the resilience and adaptability of human society in a challenging environment, and shows how communities have learned to live in harmony with—and despite—nature's challenges.

Now, let's consider the intriguing case of Macquarie Island, a subantarctic island situated halfway between New Zealand and Antarctica. This island's importance lies in its role as a haven for wildlife. Millions of seabirds nest here, alongside elephant seals and penguins, creating a vibrant and bustling ecosystem. Macquarie Island also offers a unique geological perspective, as it's one of the few places on Earth where oceanic crust rises above sea level, providing a window into Earth's geological processes. However, invasive species and the effects of climate change are presenting significant threats to this remarkable environment, highlighting the universal challenge of conservation in the face of a changing world.

Our journey wouldn't be complete without acknowledging the unique challenges facing these islands. Climate change is perhaps the most pressing concern, with rising sea levels, shifting weather patterns, and ocean acidification impacting even the most isolated environments. Invasive species, introduced inadvertently or deliberately, pose significant risks to native flora and fauna. The delicate balance of these unique ecosystems is easily disrupted, often with catastrophic consequences. Pollution, from plastic debris to chemical runoff, is also reaching these remote locations, underscoring the global nature of environmental problems. Sustainable tourism, careful resource management, and international collaboration are essential for protecting these irreplaceable islands for future generations.

Beyond the environmental challenges, many remote islands face socio-economic issues. Limited resources, economic dependence on external markets, and the challenges of providing essential services in remote locations create complex hurdles for the communities that call these islands home. Supporting sustainable development in these communities is crucial for ensuring their well-being and preserving their unique cultures. Many of these communities are intimately tied to their environment; their livelihoods directly dependent on the health of the local ecosystem. Protecting these environments is thus crucial not just for the planet, but for the well-being of the people who call them home.

The exploration of these remote and unique islands offers a profound lesson: our planet's diversity is far richer and more complex than we often realize. Each island tells a unique story, a testament to the power of nature's resilience and the ingenuity of humankind. But it also serves as a reminder of our responsibility to protect these extraordinary places and the delicate balance they represent, before their unique stories are lost forever. The preservation of these islands isn't just about safeguarding biodiversity; it's about safeguarding the future of our planet and acknowledging the intricate tapestry of life that thrives in even the most remote corners of the world. It's about preserving these precious legacies for the generations to come, so that future adventurers can continue to explore these wonders and be as awestruck as we are today. The stories of these islands, woven together by the threads of geography, culture, and conservation, form a powerful narrative, one that challenges us to appreciate the beauty of our world and act to protect its most precious treasures. The call to action is clear: we must embrace our role as custodians of these unique environments, ensuring that the tales of these islands continue to inspire and captivate for generations to come. The future of these islands, and indeed the future of our planet, hinges on our collective commitment to preserving these incredible, remote wonders.

Strange Customs & Traditions

OUR journey continues, leaving behind the isolated beauty of remote islands to explore a different kind of geographical marvel: the rich tapestry of human cultures across the globe. While islands offer a glimpse into the power of isolation shaping unique ecosystems, human societies demonstrate the fascinating diversity that arises from interaction, adaptation, and the sheer inventiveness of the human spirit. And that inventiveness often leads to traditions and customs that leave us scratching our heads, chuckling, or simply utterly bewildered. Let's delve into some of the world's most unusual cultural curiosities.

Consider, for instance, the fascinating tradition of "baby jumping" in Spain. Every year, during the festival of El Colacho, men dressed as devils leap over babies lying on mattresses in the streets. This seemingly reckless act is believed to cleanse the infants of sin and bring them good luck. While it might raise eyebrows in many parts of the world, it's a deeply ingrained tradition rooted in centuries of religious observance. It's a perfect example of how cultural norms can radically differ and why judging such practices from an outside perspective requires a considerable amount of understanding and sensitivity. This tradition isn't a malicious act; it's a cultural expression woven into the fabric of the local community. Understanding such traditions requires a move beyond the superficial and a deeper dive into the historical, social, and religious context.

Then there's the striking case of the Maasai people of East Africa, known for their vibrant culture and distinctive adornments. Their traditions often involve elaborate rituals and ceremonies that are both beautiful and deeply meaningful to them. Their age-set system, for example, divides the population into age groups, each with specific roles and responsibilities. This structure contributes to social cohesion and stability. The intricate bead-work and jewellery worn by Maasai women aren't merely decorative; they are powerful symbols of identity, status, and marital status. Each colour, pattern, and material holds significance within their cultural narrative. These adornments are not just accessories, they tell a story. They narrate a history, a social standing, a personal journey. To understand the Maasai culture, one must appreciate the intricate details embedded in their adornments – a silent language speaking volumes about their societal structure. The apparent simplicity of beads hides a complex system of meaning.

Moving to Asia, we encounter the incredible tradition of the "baby throwing festival" in Castrillo de Murcia, Spain. This unique celebration, again, involves babies being thrown from a church tower, but unlike the Spanish baby jumping tradition, the babies are caught by adults holding a blanket below. The tradition is considered a form of blessing. Here, the concept of risk is intertwined with faith, showcasing the different ways cultures express their beliefs. But it's crucial to remember that these are not actions taken lightly; there is years of practice and preparation that goes into ensuring the safety of these tiny participants, though the perceived risk remains a fascinating aspect of this celebration. It serves as a stark reminder of cultural norms that might seem bizarre or even dangerous from an outsider's perspective.

Across the Pacific Ocean, we find the intriguing custom of "yam cultivation" in certain Pacific Island cultures. Yams aren't just a staple food; they hold deep symbolic and cultural significance. In some communities, the size and quality of a person's yam harvest reflect their social standing and status. The cultivation and harvesting of yams are often accompanied by elaborate ceremonies and rituals. This isn't merely about farming; it's about community, social hierarchy, and spirituality, all wrapped into a single activity. The connection between humans and the land, the respect for nature, and the importance of community are deeply woven into these traditions. This again highlights how an everyday activity can be imbued with profound cultural and spiritual meaning.

Delving into the heart of Asia, we uncover the remarkable cultural phenomena surrounding the consumption of insects. In many parts of the continent, insects are a common source of protein, and their culinary uses are incredibly diverse. From fried grasshoppers to grilled crickets, the variety of insect dishes is astounding. These practices, while perhaps unsettling to some Western palates, reflect a sustainable and resourceful approach to food production. Furthermore, this tradition underscores the vast differences in culinary preferences and food cultures across the world. What one culture might consider a delicacy, another might view with disgust. This reinforces the concept of cultural relativism, highlighting the importance of appreciating diverse culinary traditions without judgment. The nutritional value and sustainability aspects of entomophagy are increasingly attracting the attention of global researchers.

From the vibrant celebrations of Holi in India, where people playfully throw coloured powders and water at each other, to the solemn traditions of the Day of the Dead in Mexico, where families gather to remember and honour deceased loved ones, human customs paint a striking picture of our planet's rich cultural diversity. The symbolic significance of colours in Holi, the artistry and spiritual connection present in the Day of the Dead altars, these are only but a few examples of how cultures creatively express their beliefs, values, and histories.

The seemingly bizarre tradition of spitting to show respect in certain parts of the world stands as a striking example. While it might appear disrespectful to those unfamiliar with the practice, it often stems from a deeply rooted cultural belief that embodies good luck or even admiration. It reminds us that cultural interpretations, like language, can be diverse and context-specific. The act is not meant to be an affront; rather, it represents a unique form of communication within specific cultural frameworks.

Another interesting cultural practice to explore is the widespread tradition of gift-giving during festivals and celebrations. While the specifics of the gifts and rituals vary widely depending on the culture and occasion, the underlying principle remains consistent: the strengthening of social bonds and expressing goodwill. The exchange of gifts transcends geographical boundaries and acts as a universal expression of human connection. From lavish wedding gifts to modest holiday presents, the practice shows a common human desire to create and maintain social bonds through gestures of generosity.

Let's not forget the age-old tradition of storytelling. Passed down through generations, these narratives often transmit important cultural values, beliefs, and historical accounts. The use of elaborate costumes, symbolic gestures, and music during the storytelling process transforms the activity into a vibrant form of cultural preservation. Every story, no matter how seemingly simple, carries within it layers of meaning, reflecting the richness of the culture it comes from.

In parts of Southeast Asia, the custom of leaving offerings at shrines or sacred sites reveals a deep spiritual connection with the natural world. These offerings, which vary from food and flowers to incense and money, serve as expressions of reverence and gratitude. This practice, while distinct from Western customs, highlights how different cultures express their spiritual beliefs and interactions with the divine. Understanding the significance of these offerings allows for a deeper appreciation of the reverence for ancestral spirits and the interconnectedness between humanity and nature within specific cultural contexts.

Finally, the varied customs surrounding marriage ceremonies across the globe showcase the diversity of human relationships and societal structures. From lavish arranged marriages to intimate elopements, the practices reflect the unique values and beliefs prevalent within different cultures. The diversity of traditions associated with marriage ceremonies, including the role of family, the significance of gifts, and the importance of religious or spiritual elements, offers a fascinating insight into the diverse ways human beings form and celebrate lifelong partnerships. These differences are not simply arbitrary; they represent a deep reflection of values, social structures, and cultural beliefs within each society.

In conclusion, exploring global cultural customs reveals a breathtaking spectrum of human ingenuity, resilience, and adaptability. While some customs might seem unusual or even perplexing to outsiders, understanding their historical, social, and religious contexts is crucial to appreciating their significance within their specific cultures. This exploration challenges us to look beyond our own cultural lenses and embrace the vast diversity of human experience. It's a reminder that our planet's richness lies not just in its geographical diversity, but also in the countless ways humans have interacted with their environment and each other, shaping unique and vibrant traditions that have endured through time. The continued exploration and understanding of these cultural curiosities enrich our global perspectives and promote inter-cultural understanding and respect. The journey of discovery never ends.

Natures Unexpected Masterpieces

OUR journey into the unexpected continues, shifting our gaze from the vibrant tapestry of human cultures to the equally astonishing and often bewildering wonders of the natural world. While human ingenuity has shaped societies in remarkable ways, the Earth itself has been sculpting breathtaking landscapes for millennia, creating geographical anomalies that defy easy explanation and leave us marvelling at the sheer power of nature. These are not your typical textbook landscapes; these are the outliers, the geological oddities, the unexpected masterpieces sculpted by wind, water, ice, and fire.

Let's start with the surreal beauty of the Salar de Uyuni in Bolivia, the world's largest salt flat. Imagine a landscape stretching as far as the eye can see, a blinding expanse of white, reflecting the sky in such a way that it creates the illusion of an endless mirror. This seemingly barren landscape was once a prehistoric lake, its waters slowly evaporating over millions of years, leaving behind a crust of salt several meters thick. During the rainy season, it transforms into a shallow lake, reflecting the sky with such pristine clarity that it becomes a photographer's paradise and a testament to nature's dramatic transformations. But beyond the stunning visuals, the Salar de Uyuni holds vast reserves of lithium, a crucial element in modern battery technology – a modern twist to this ancient geological wonder. The scale alone is mind-boggling; it covers an area larger than some countries. To wander across it is to experience a sense of utter isolation and overwhelming vastness, a humbling reminder of the Earth's immense power.

Then there's the breathtaking spectacle of the Giant's Causeway in Northern Ireland. This dramatic coastline is composed of approximately 40,000 interlocking basalt columns, the result of an ancient volcanic eruption. These columns, mostly hexagonal but with some exhibiting four, five, seven, or eight sides, are remarkably uniform in shape, creating a mesmerizing pattern that looks almost artificially constructed. Legend tells of a giant, Finn MacCool, who built the causeway to reach Scotland, a charming narrative that adds to the site's mystique. The reality, however, is far more intriguing; the columns are the result of a slow cooling process of lava flows, creating the unique geometric formations we see today. It's a geological puzzle box, showcasing the intricate processes occurring deep beneath the Earth's surface. And the dramatic contrast of the dark basalt columns against the churning Atlantic Ocean is a sight that will leave you speechless.

Moving to the subterranean wonders, we encounter the Carlsbad Caverns in New Mexico, a subterranean labyrinth of dazzling formations. These colossal caves, carved out of limestone by the patient work of groundwater over millions of years, boast magnificent stalactites hanging from the ceilings and stalagmites rising from the floors, some reaching immense heights. The sheer scale and intricate detail of these formations are astonishing, a testament to the powerful, slow sculpting effects of nature's patient hand. The caves are not merely aesthetically pleasing; they are also a home to a unique ecosystem, harbouring several species of bats and other cave-dwelling creatures, adapted to survive in this unique, dark environment. Exploring these caves is like stepping into another world, a realm of breathtaking beauty and geological mystery.

The underwater world also provides its share of geographical wonders. The Great Barrier Reef, off the coast of Australia, is the world's largest coral reef system, a vibrant and biodiverse ecosystem visible from space. Millions of individual coral polyps construct this underwater metropolis, creating a spectacular underwater landscape of unimaginable beauty and complexity. Its vastness is awe-inspiring, and the sheer number of species it supports is staggering. However, this breathtaking wonder is under threat from climate change and pollution, highlighting the fragility of these delicate ecosystems and the importance of conservation efforts. The vibrant colours and the sheer abundance of life on the reef present a powerful reminder of the importance of preserving this extraordinary natural wonder.

And let's not forget the dramatic landscapes carved by glaciers. Glacial valleys, like Yosemite Valley in California, are testaments to the immense power of ice. These U-shaped valleys, sculpted by the relentless movement of glaciers, are characterized by their steep, almost vertical walls and flat floors. The sheer scale of these formations speaks volumes about the power of these colossal ice rivers, shaping landscapes in profound ways. Yosemite Valley, with its iconic granite cliffs, waterfalls, and giant sequoia trees, is a breathtaking example of the beauty that can arise from the erosive power of glaciers.

The list of geographical wonders could go on and on: the Zhangjiajie National Forest Park in China, with its towering sandstone pillars that inspired the landscape of Pandora in Avatar; the eerie beauty of the Socotra archipelago, with its alien-like flora; the towering cliffs of the Norwegian fjords, carved by ancient glaciers; the otherworldly landscapes of Iceland, shaped by volcanic activity and glaciers; the underwater canyons of the Pacific Ocean, with their rich biodiversity. Each of these locations stands as a testament to the dynamic forces that shape our planet, showcasing the remarkable diversity of landscapes and ecosystems found across the globe.

The exploration of these geographical wonders is not simply a pursuit of aesthetic appreciation. It's a journey into the heart of our planet's history, a chance to witness the powerful forces that have shaped its surface over millions of years. These locations serve as reminders of the planet's incredible power and the delicate balance of its ecosystems. They also underscore the importance of conservation efforts to protect these unique and valuable natural resources for future generations. The beauty and strangeness of these landscapes offer a profound sense of wonder, reminding us of the planet's immense beauty and the importance of understanding and protecting it. From the crystalline salt flats of Bolivia to the volcanic rock formations of Ireland, these geographical wonders are reminders of Earth's artistic capabilities, far surpassing any human creation in both scale and spectacle. They challenge us to look beyond the familiar, to appreciate the unexpected, and to acknowledge the power and beauty of a planet that continues to surprise and amaze. Our exploration into the unexpected continues, ever revealing more of nature's artistic mastery, demonstrating the exquisite artistry of geological processes and the extraordinary adaptability of life on Earth. Each location is a unique testament to the power of natural processes, providing captivating insights into the Earth's dynamic past and present. These geographical marvels are not merely scenic attractions; they are living testaments to the ongoing creation and evolution of our planet, rich in scientific significance and offering invaluable opportunities for understanding Earth's geological and ecological history. They highlight the crucial interplay between geological forces and biodiversity, showcasing the fragile beauty of these unique ecosystems. The continuing research and study of these wonders are essential for better understanding the planet's geological processes and protecting these valuable resources for the future.

The study of geographical wonders also extends beyond their aesthetic value; they provide crucial scientific data on geological processes, climate change impacts, and biodiversity. The patterns in the Giant's Causeway offer valuable insights into volcanic activity, while the Salar de Uyuni's lithium reserves are vital to our technological advancement. Understanding these locations helps us understand the broader geological and ecological contexts, enabling better prediction of future events, and informing more effective conservation strategies. Furthermore, the unique ecosystems found in these areas often support unique species and flora, adding to our understanding of biodiversity and its importance. Studying and preserving these locations are vital not just for their beauty but also for their scientific importance and contribution to our understanding of the Earth. They are living laboratories, providing ongoing opportunities for research and discovery.

Finally, let us not forget the profound impact these geographical wonders have on human cultures. Many are associated with myths and legends, reflecting the ways humans have interacted with and interpreted these remarkable landscapes. The Giant's Causeway, for example, is steeped in folklore, highlighting the creative and imaginative ways humans have engaged with their surroundings. These stories are not simply fanciful tales; they are expressions of human interaction with the environment, reflecting our awe, curiosity, and attempts to understand the world around us. The preservation of these geographical wonders is therefore not just a matter of protecting the environment, but also of safeguarding cultural heritage, the stories and traditions woven into the fabric of these landscapes. The ongoing efforts to protect and preserve these wonders are crucial not just for ecological reasons, but also for ensuring the continuation of cultural narratives and the preservation of human connection to the natural world. The integration of these geographical wonders into tourism strategies must balance the economic opportunities with the crucial need for environmental protection and the preservation of the cultural significance of these sites. A sustainable approach is essential, ensuring these wonders remain accessible for generations to come while preserving their ecological integrity and cultural heritage. The ultimate goal is to ensure that future generations can also experience the awe and wonder that these remarkable places evoke.

The Worlds Most Unusual Languages

OUR exploration of the planet's wonders now shifts from the breathtaking landscapes sculpted by nature to the equally fascinating landscapes shaped by human ingenuity: language. While mountains and canyons speak volumes about geological processes, languages offer a window into the vibrant tapestry of human history, culture, and thought. Just as geographical features defy easy categorization, so too do the world's languages, boasting a breathtaking diversity that reflects the ingenuity and adaptability of humankind. We're venturing beyond the familiar tongues of English, Spanish, or Mandarin, to unearth linguistic gems that challenge our assumptions about communication, showcasing the remarkable adaptability and creativity of the human mind. Prepare to be amazed by linguistic quirks that are as unexpected as a geyser erupting in the middle of the desert.

Let's begin with the languages that seem to defy grammatical logic, those that play with sounds and structures in ways that leave linguists scratching their heads. Consider Pirahã, spoken by a small tribe in the Amazon rainforest. This language is famously minimalist, lacking numbers, quantifiers, and even a concept of colour. Its grammar is strikingly different from most languages, leading to debates about the very nature of language itself. Does its simplicity reflect a different way of perceiving the world? Or does it simply highlight the enormous diversity possible within human communication? The answer remains elusive, adding to the mystery and intrigue of this fascinating tongue. Understanding Pirahã, with its almost alien grammar and vocabulary, prompts a reconsideration of our own assumptions about how language works and the very nature of thought itself.

Then there are languages that confound us with their complex sound systems. Click languages of Southern Africa, such as Xhosa and !Xóõ, incorporate clicks – sounds made by sucking air into the mouth – as integral parts of their phonology. Imagine a language where the sound of a kiss or a gentle suction becomes a crucial element of word formation! Mastering these languages requires a dexterity of the mouth and tongue that many speakers of other languages can only dream of. These clicks aren't merely decorative; they carry distinct meaning and grammatical function. The existence of click languages challenges our preconceptions about the range of sounds humans can produce and use for communication, pushing the boundaries of what we consider 'normal' speech. Learning these languages offers a deep dive into an auditory world utterly different from our own, a testament to the human capacity for vocal innovation.

The visual landscape of language is equally captivating. Consider the writing systems themselves. While many languages use alphabets based on representing individual sounds, others employ logographic systems, where each symbol represents a whole word or morpheme. Chinese, for example, is a prime example of this, with thousands of characters to memorize. Imagine the cognitive effort required to master such a writing system! It's a far cry from the relatively simple 26-letter alphabet used in English. The sheer visual complexity of these scripts is a testament to the power of human visual processing. These languages aren't just systems of communication; they are intricate visual puzzles that reveal much about the cultural values and cognitive capacities of their users.

Even within seemingly familiar linguistic families, unexpected quirks can be found. Take the case of grammatical gender. While many Indo-European languages assign grammatical gender to nouns (masculine, feminine, neuter), some languages take this concept to extremes. For example, some languages in Africa categorize nouns according to far more nuanced criteria, extending beyond simple binary categories to encompass various social and cultural classifications. The very concept of grammatical gender itself takes on a profound socio-cultural significance, reflecting deep-seated cultural values and worldviews. This shows that grammatical gender is not merely a linguistic convention but can become a powerful tool to reflect and embed social hierarchies and structures in the very fabric of the language itself.

Furthermore, consider languages that challenge our notions of word order. In English, the typical order is Subject-Verb-Object (SVO). However, some languages employ vastly different word orders, such as Subject-Object-Verb (SOV) or Verb-Subject-Object (VSO). These differences affect not just the surface structure of sentences, but also deeper aspects of how information is presented and interpreted. The way a language organizes its sentences is a window into the cognitive processes underlying how its speakers understand and express themselves. It is a reflection of how they make sense of the world and structure their thought processes around grammar itself. Studying these variations expands our understanding of cognitive flexibility and how the structure of language shapes our thought.

Moreover, let's not forget the languages that are constantly evolving, adapting, and incorporating elements from other languages. Creole languages, for instance, often arise from the contact between different linguistic communities. These languages are born out of necessity, acting as a common ground for communication among diverse populations. They often blend grammatical structures and vocabulary from their parent languages in unexpected and fascinating ways, creating unique linguistic entities with their own distinct character and identity. The creation of Creole languages is a dynamic testament to language's ability to adapt and serve as a medium of communication across cultural boundaries.

Linguistic diversity is not merely an academic curiosity; it's a reflection of the rich tapestry of human experience. Each language carries within it a wealth of cultural knowledge, historical context, and unique ways of understanding the world. The loss of a language is not just the loss of words and grammar; it's the loss of an entire cultural heritage, a unique perspective on life. The preservation of linguistic diversity is therefore crucial, not only for academic reasons but also for safeguarding the cultural heritage of countless communities around the globe. The survival of these unique languages is not just a linguistic endeavour, but an urgent call to protect cultural diversity in all its forms. It's a testament to the immense creativity and adaptability of the human race.

This intricate dance of sounds, grammar, and visual representation paints a vivid picture of the world's linguistic landscape. The languages discussed here represent just a tiny fraction of the incredible diversity that exists. From the minimalist Pirahã to the click languages of Africa, each language offers a unique perspective on the world, a unique window into the human mind, and a testament to the power of human communication and creativity. The study of these linguistic landscapes is not just an academic exercise; it is a journey of discovery, a celebration of human ingenuity, and a reminder of the interconnectedness of language, culture, and the human experience. As we delve into these intricate linguistic worlds, we gain a deeper appreciation for the sheer complexity and beauty of human language and its vital role in shaping our understanding of ourselves and the world around us. The continued study and preservation of these languages are not only essential for scientific knowledge, but also for the enrichment of human understanding and appreciation for the intricate diversity of human experience. These linguistic gems are priceless treasures, reflecting the extraordinary capacity for innovation and expression that is uniquely human. Their preservation is not simply a matter of academic interest; it is a matter of safeguarding a crucial part of our collective heritage. The beauty and complexity of these languages are truly breathtaking and serve as an inspirational reminder of the unbounded potential of human creativity and ingenuity.

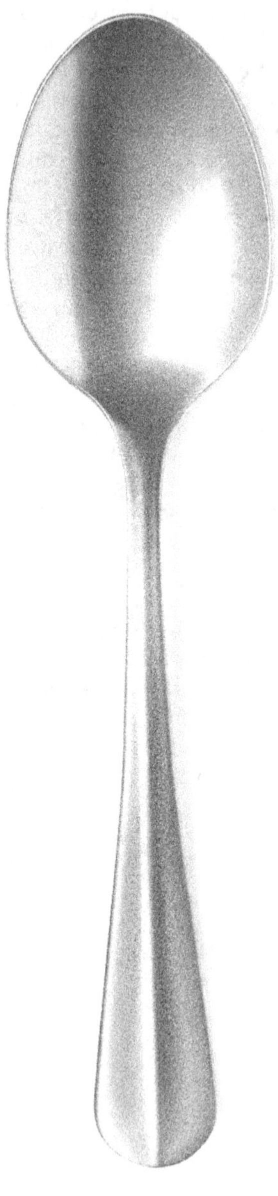

The Worlds Most Unusual Foods

OUR journey continues, shifting from the intricacies of language to another fascinating facet of global culture: food. While languages shape our communication, cuisine reflects our history, environment, and ingenuity in a truly mouth-watering (or sometimes, stomach-churning) way. Forget your predictable pizzas and burgers; we're diving head first into the world of culinary curiosities, exploring dishes so unusual they'll make you question everything you thought you knew about gastronomy.

Prepare yourself for a whirlwind tour of edible oddities, from the seemingly repulsive to the surprisingly delicious. We'll encounter delicacies that challenge our preconceived notions of taste and texture, reminding us that culinary preferences are as diverse and fascinating as the languages we explored in the previous chapter. Consider, for example, the humble durian. This spiky, pungent fruit, native to Southeast Asia, is notorious for its overwhelmingly strong odour, often described as a combination of gym socks, turpentine, and rotting onions. Yet, to millions across Southeast Asia, it's a prized delicacy, celebrated for its creamy texture and surprisingly sweet flavour. The aroma alone is enough to clear a room in many Western supermarkets, yet in its native land, it's enjoyed fresh, in ice cream, and even in savoury dishes. This stark contrast perfectly illustrates the cultural relativity of taste; what repels one culture can be a beloved treasure in another.

Let's travel further afield to discover the culinary delights (and challenges) of Iceland. Hákarl, a traditional Icelandic dish made from fermented Greenland shark, is notorious for its potent ammonia smell and intensely strong flavour, which some describe as being similar to a mixture of urine and cleaning products. The fermentation process, which can take months or even years, is essential to remove toxins naturally present in the shark meat. While not for the faint of heart, Hákarl is a testament to Icelandic resourcefulness and a unique example of how necessity and tradition can shape a nation's culinary landscape. It's a dish that embodies the saying, "One man's trash is another man's treasure," taken to an extreme level. The enduring popularity of Hákarl among Icelanders highlights the deep cultural ties associated with food, its preparation, and its consumption. The dish is more than just a meal; it's a ritual, a tradition, and a symbol of Icelandic identity.

Moving on to the Amazon, we encounter insects, not as pests, but as a valuable source of protein. Ants, grasshoppers, and beetles are common ingredients in many Amazonian dishes, often roasted, fried, or even incorporated into sauces. These insect-based dishes are not only a sustainable food source but also a significant part of the local culture and traditions. The practice of entomophagy (eating insects) is prevalent in many parts of the world, highlighting the versatility of insects as a food source and challenging Western biases against insect consumption. Consider, for instance, the escamoles, or ant larvae, a highly prized delicacy in Mexico, often described as having a buttery, nutty flavour. The price of escamoles reflects their scarcity and high demand; they're often more expensive than other protein sources, demonstrating that the concept of culinary value is far from universal.

From the Americas to Asia, our culinary journey takes us to China, where we encounter a delicacy that truly tests the boundaries of the palatable: balut. Balut is a fertilized duck egg that is boiled and eaten while the embryo is still developing. This dish, popular in the Philippines and parts of Southeast Asia, is often consumed as a street food, readily available from vendors across various regions. While the visual aspect might be off-putting to many Westerners, the taste is described by some as having a rich and savoury flavour, the yolk resembling a creamy custard-like consistency. Balut's widespread popularity underlines the complex relationship between culture and food preferences, showcasing how cultural norms significantly impact the perception of specific foods. It's a dish that forces us to confront our own biases and consider the diversity of culinary traditions around the world.

Our culinary odyssey wouldn't be complete without mentioning the fascinating world of fermented foods. From the pungent kimchi of Korea to the creamy surströmming (fermented herring) of Sweden, fermented foods play a crucial role in many cultures, not only for their unique flavors but also for their nutritional value and preservation properties. Surströmming, often considered one of the world's smelliest foods, requires special handling due to its potent odour, which can linger for weeks after opening the can. Yet, despite its pungent aroma, surströmming is a treasured delicacy in Sweden, and its distinctive flavour is deeply intertwined with Swedish culinary heritage. It's a testament to the fact that culinary tastes are often strongly influenced by cultural norms and traditions, and that what one culture considers repulsive, another might relish.

The culinary landscapes of the world are as diverse and complex as the geographical landscapes we explored earlier. From the seemingly repulsive to the undeniably delicious, these unusual foods challenge our perceptions of taste and broaden our understanding of cultural diversity. They highlight the significant role of food in shaping cultural identities and the intricate interplay between tradition, innovation, and resourcefulness in the creation of culinary traditions. The next time you reach for your familiar comfort food, take a moment to appreciate the incredible variety of culinary experiences that exist globally, and perhaps even dare to step outside your comfort zone to try something truly unique. The rewards—both culinary and cultural—are well worth the adventure.

The diversity of culinary practices globally demonstrates the human capacity for innovation and adaptation. Culinary traditions frequently reflect not only environmental factors but also a society's economic realities, historical events, and cultural values. The utilization of unusual ingredients, such as insects or fermented products, often points to resourcefulness and sustainability, reminding us that culinary practices are a key component of a civilization's survival and cultural identity. The persistence of these unique culinary traditions provides a compelling testament to the resilience and adaptiveness of human societies. These customs also serve as a crucial link to the past, offering insights into the history and cultural development of various communities. They remind us that gastronomy is not merely sustenance; it's a vibrant tapestry woven from the threads of history, environment, and ingenuity.

This culinary journey, though brief, underscores the intricate relationship between food and culture. The dishes we've discussed are more than just food; they are symbols, traditions, and stories that reveal the rich tapestry of human experience. They force us to confront our own biases and appreciate the diversity of culinary customs around the world. The next time you sit down to a meal, remember the extraordinary range of edible experiences that exist—from the delicate flavours of haute cuisine to the pungent aromas of fermented delicacies. Each bite tells a story, a story of culture, history, and human ingenuity. And perhaps, just perhaps, it will inspire you to step outside your culinary comfort zone and discover a new world of flavours, aromas, and cultural insights. This culinary exploration only scratches the surface of global culinary diversity. Countless other unusual and intriguing dishes exist, waiting to be discovered and savoured. The world of food is a vast and exciting one, full of surprises and adventures for those willing to embrace the unknown. So, bon appétit, and may your next culinary adventure be as surprising and rewarding as the ones we've explored here.

The preservation of these unique culinary traditions is of paramount importance. Globalization and modernization often pose threats to traditional practices, leading to the loss of cultural heritage and culinary diversity. The continuation of these food traditions ensures not only the survival of unique flavours and preparations but also safeguards invaluable aspects of cultural history and knowledge. The passing down of culinary expertise through generations serves as a potent link to the past, maintaining cultural identity, and promoting a deeper appreciation for the richness of human history and cultural heritage. The significance of these traditions extends beyond the individual to encompass the collective cultural memory of communities, highlighting the interconnectedness of culinary practices and cultural preservation.

Therefore, appreciating and supporting these unusual foods and their associated cultures becomes more than merely a matter of culinary exploration; it is an act of preserving valuable cultural heritage, a commitment to preserving the diversity of global gastronomy, and a celebration of human ingenuity. By understanding the cultural significance of these culinary practices, we foster a greater understanding and appreciation of the world's cultural landscape, enhancing cross-cultural interactions, and promoting a more nuanced and respectful global community. So, the next time you encounter a dish that seems strange or unfamiliar, remember the rich history and cultural significance behind it, and approach it with an open mind and a curious palate. You might just discover a new favourite, and in doing so, contribute to the preservation of a precious piece of culinary heritage.

Unravelling the Mysteries of Dreams

We spend roughly a third of our lives doing it — a nightly ritual as regular as the sunrise, yet shrouded in more mystery than a locked Egyptian tomb. Sleep: that blissful, often elusive state where consciousness dips below the surface, leaving us vulnerable to the whims of the subconscious and the bizarre landscapes of dreams. But beyond the simple act of closing our eyes and drifting off, there's a complex symphony of neurological activity, hormonal fluctuations, and physiological processes at play. It's a realm scientists are still actively exploring, piecing together the puzzle of sleep's importance and the enigma of dreams.

One of the most fascinating aspects of sleep is its multi-stage nature. It's not just one homogenous state of unconsciousness. Instead, we cycle through various stages throughout the night, each with its own distinct characteristics and functions. Non-REM sleep, for instance, is divided into three stages, progressing from light sleep (stage 1) to progressively deeper sleep (stages 2 and 3). During these stages, our heart rate slows, our breathing becomes more regular, and our brain waves shift from the fast, erratic activity of wakefulness to slower, more rhythmic patterns. This deep sleep is crucial for physical restoration — repairing tissues, replenishing energy stores, and releasing growth hormones. Did you know that a lack of deep sleep can actually impair your immune system, making you more susceptible to illness? Now you do!

Then comes the grand finale of the sleep cycle: REM (Rapid Eye Movement) sleep. This is where things get truly bizarre. Characterized by rapid eye movements behind closed eyelids, increased brain activity comparable to wakefulness, and vivid dreaming, REM sleep is thought to play a critical role in memory consolidation and emotional processing. The brainwaves during REM sleep are strikingly similar to those during wakefulness, a curious parallel that hints at the complex interplay between consciousness and unconsciousness. During REM, your body is essentially paralyzed, preventing you from acting out your dreams (unless you have a rare sleep disorder, of course!). This fascinating safeguard ensures you don't accidentally embody your dream-self and attempt to fly through your bedroom window.

And what about those dreams themselves? The kaleidoscopic visions, bizarre narratives, and sometimes intensely emotional experiences that populate the nightly landscape of our minds. For centuries, dreams have been interpreted as messages from the gods, premonitions of the future, or simply the random firing of neurons. Modern neuroscience offers a more nuanced perspective, suggesting that dreams are a byproduct of the brain's attempts to process information, consolidate memories, and regulate emotions. The chaotic jumble of images and story-lines, therefore, might be the brain's way of making sense of the day's experiences, sifting through memories, and resolving emotional conflicts.

Consider this: a study found that people who learned a new skill, like solving a puzzle, were more likely to dream about it later. This lends credence to the idea that dreams are involved in consolidating what we've learned. They may even help us problem-solve. How many times have you woken up with a solution to a nagging issue, a flash of inspiration stemming from the depths of your dreamworld? While some dreams are mundane and easily forgotten, others leave a lasting impression, their images and emotions lingering long after we awaken.

Sleep deprivation, on the other hand, is not a fun adventure. It affects almost every aspect of our lives. It impairs cognitive functions such as attention, memory, and decision-making. It can also have a profound impact on our mood, increasing irritability, anxiety, and even depression. Chronic sleep deprivation has been linked to an increased risk of various health problems, including obesity, cardiovascular disease, and even certain types of cancer. The importance of sleep cannot be overstated; it's the bedrock of physical and mental health.

But why do we dream? The mystery continues to intrigue scientists. While the exact function of dreams remains elusive, several compelling theories exist. The activation-synthesis theory suggests that dreams are the brain's attempt to make sense of random neural activity during REM sleep, essentially creating a narrative from the noise. Other theories emphasize the role of dreams in emotional processing, suggesting that they allow us to work through anxieties, fears, and unresolved conflicts in a safe, virtual environment. One could even say that dreams are the brain's nightly therapy session.

The content of our dreams is often profoundly personal, reflecting our individual experiences, fears, and desires. Recurring dreams, in particular, can offer valuable insights into our subconscious thoughts and emotional patterns. They may highlight unresolved issues or recurring anxieties that need attention. Analysing your dreams can feel like deciphering an ancient code – challenging, rewarding, and sometimes unsettling.

Moreover, the study of dreams has captivated humans for millennia, influencing art, literature, and psychology. From ancient Egyptian dream books to Freud's psychoanalytic interpretations, the quest to understand the meaning and purpose of dreams has been a constant thread in human history. The very act of recalling and interpreting dreams is a form of self-reflection, a journey into the hidden depths of our own minds. It's no wonder that dream analysis continues to be a powerful tool in psychotherapy, helping individuals explore and understand their emotional landscape.

Beyond the individual experience, the science of sleep also touches on broader societal issues. Sleep disorders, such as insomnia, sleep apnoea, and narcolepsy, affect millions worldwide, impacting their quality of life and productivity. Understanding the causes and treatments of these disorders is critical for improving public health. The societal implications are immense, ranging from decreased workplace performance to increased healthcare costs.

Then there's the intriguing world of lucid dreaming, where individuals become aware that they are dreaming and can, to some extent, control the narrative and environment of their dream. While still an area of active research, lucid dreaming is gaining traction as a potential tool for therapeutic interventions, helping individuals confront their fears and practice coping mechanisms in a safe, dream-like setting. Imagine facing your worst nightmare, not in the grip of terror, but consciously and in control – that's the potential of lucid dreaming.

The study of sleep and dreams is far from complete. New research continually reveals deeper layers of complexity, adding to the intrigue and mystery. We are only beginning to grasp the full extent of sleep's importance for our physical and mental health, the role of dreams in our emotional lives, and the potential of dream research to unlock further understanding of the human brain. The next time you drift off to sleep, remember the fascinating journey your mind is embarking on, a nightly expedition into the hidden landscapes of your own consciousness. The world of dreams is indeed a mystery worth unravelling. Sweet dreams!

Unexpected Innovations

WE'VE journeyed through the enigmatic world of sleep, delving into its mysteries and marvels. Now, let's shift gears and explore another realm of fascinating unpredictability: the world of inventions and innovations. History is littered with breakthroughs that weren't necessarily planned, meticulously researched outcomes, but rather happy accidents, serendipitous discoveries, or solutions born out of necessity—sometimes even sheer desperation. These unexpected inventions have profoundly shaped our lives, often in ways their creators could never have imagined.

Take, for example, the humble microwave oven. Its story isn't one of a visionary scientist toiling away in a lab, but rather a rather peculiar observation made by Percy Spencer, an engineer working with magnetrons—devices used in radar technology during World War II. Spencer noticed a chocolate bar in his pocket melting inexplicably near an active magnetron. This seemingly insignificant incident sparked an idea: Could this electromagnetic radiation be used to cook food? The rest, as they say, is history. The microwave oven, born from a melted chocolate bar, is now a staple in kitchens worldwide, a testament to the power of accidental discovery.

Similarly, the discovery of penicillin, the wonder drug that revolutionized medicine, was far from a carefully orchestrated experiment. Alexander Fleming, a Scottish bacteriologist, left a petri dish of Staphylococcus bacteria unattended during a vacation. Upon returning, he noticed that a mould had contaminated the dish, and astonishingly, the bacteria surrounding the mould had been destroyed. This accidental observation led to the isolation and identification of penicillin, a breakthrough that has saved countless lives, a true testament to the serendipity of scientific investigation. It's a reminder that sometimes, the most significant discoveries are stumbled upon rather than meticulously planned.

Let's not forget the invention of Post-it notes. Spencer Silver, a 3M scientist, was trying to develop a strong adhesive, but he instead created a weak, reusable one. For years, it seemed like a failed experiment, a dead end in the research process. However, his colleague Art Fry, frustrated with bookmarks falling out of his hymnal during church services, had a lightbulb moment. He realized Silver's "failed" adhesive was perfect for creating reusable notes. Thus, the Post-it note was born, proving that what is considered a failure in one context can be a ground-breaking success in another. The story underscores that the line between failure and success is often surprisingly thin.

The story of Teflon, another ubiquitous material found in countless applications, is similarly intriguing. Roy Plunkett, a chemist working for DuPont, was experimenting with refrigerants in 1938. He found that a gas cylinder he had been using was heavier than expected. Upon inspection, he discovered a white, waxy substance that was extremely slippery and non-reactive. This unexpected byproduct, initially deemed a nuisance, turned out to be polytetrafluoroethylene (PTFE), otherwise known as Teflon – the non-stick coating that has transformed cookware and numerous other industries. It is a perfect example of how serendipity can lead to major breakthroughs.

The discovery of X-rays also presents a classic case of accidental discovery. Wilhelm Conrad Röntgen, a German physicist, was experimenting with cathode rays in 1895 when he noticed a fluorescent screen glowing even when the tube was shielded. This mysterious radiation, which he named X-rays, was initially baffling, but it quickly proved invaluable in medical imaging. The technology changed the face of medicine dramatically, allowing for non-invasive visualization of the body's internal structures. This again highlights the unexpected nature of scientific discovery.

Even seemingly simple inventions can have unexpectedly complex origins. Consider the safety pin. While the basic concept of a fastening device with a clasp to hold it secure is ancient, the specific design of the modern safety pin, with its spring clasp, is credited to Walter Hunt in 1849. He reportedly conceived the design during a period of financial distress, needing a fast solution to create and sell a product rapidly to alleviate his debt. This invention, born out of necessity, shows that problem-solving under pressure can yield surprisingly useful results. And who knew a small spring could make such a big difference?

Similarly, the invention of the zipper also contains some unusual details in its genesis. Early versions of fastening mechanisms existed, but the modern zipper, that ubiquitous fastening device that holds our clothing together, took a few decades to evolve. The combination of interlocking teeth and a slider was a brilliant, and ultimately convenient solution, though its earliest incarnations were not known for their strength. This journey from a rough idea to the reliable technology we use daily is a tale of gradual refinement and innovation. It wasn't a single "eureka" moment but rather a series of improvements and innovations.

The list of serendipitous inventions and innovations extends far beyond these examples. The vulcanization of rubber, the development of dynamite, the discovery of radioactivity – all share stories of unexpected twists and turns. In many cases, these pivotal moments were not the result of years of focused research and a clearly defined goal, but rather unintended consequences, happy accidents, or unexpected observations. These instances highlight the often-overlooked role of chance encounters and intuitive leaps in the history of invention. Many significant inventions were made not in a controlled laboratory setting, but in a moment of sudden realization, sparking an idea that fundamentally changed the world.

Beyond the scientific realm, the influence of serendipity extends into other areas of invention and innovation. Consider the evolution of the printing press – an innovation initially developed for religious purposes, which subsequently transformed communication and knowledge dissemination on a global scale. Or think of the internet, initially conceived as a military communication network, which has revolutionized the way we interact, learn, and communicate in the modern world. The unforeseen capabilities and applications of these inventions far exceeded their initial intentions.

Moreover, the impact of these accidental inventions is also shaped by external factors, which in turn add another layer of fascinating complexity to the narrative. The acceptance and adoption of a novel invention are rarely predetermined, but rather influenced by cultural factors, economic forces, and technological constraints. A ground-breaking invention might fail to take off if the timing is wrong, the market is unready, or the necessary infrastructure is not in place. Thus, the success story of an invention often depends on a confluence of factors, including its inherent merit, the social climate, and pure chance.

The history of inventions and innovations is filled with stories of unexpected discoveries and unintended consequences. These stories remind us that the path to progress is rarely linear, predictable, or solely reliant on meticulous planning. There's a significant element of serendipity involved, highlighting the critical role of curiosity, observation, and the courage to explore unforeseen avenues. Sometimes, the greatest breakthroughs come not from a grand design, but from a simple, happy accident—a melted chocolate bar, a mouldy petri dish, or a sticky mishap. Each of these seemingly insignificant events has shaped the world we live in today in unexpected and extraordinary ways, underlining the surprising and often unpredictable nature of invention and innovation.

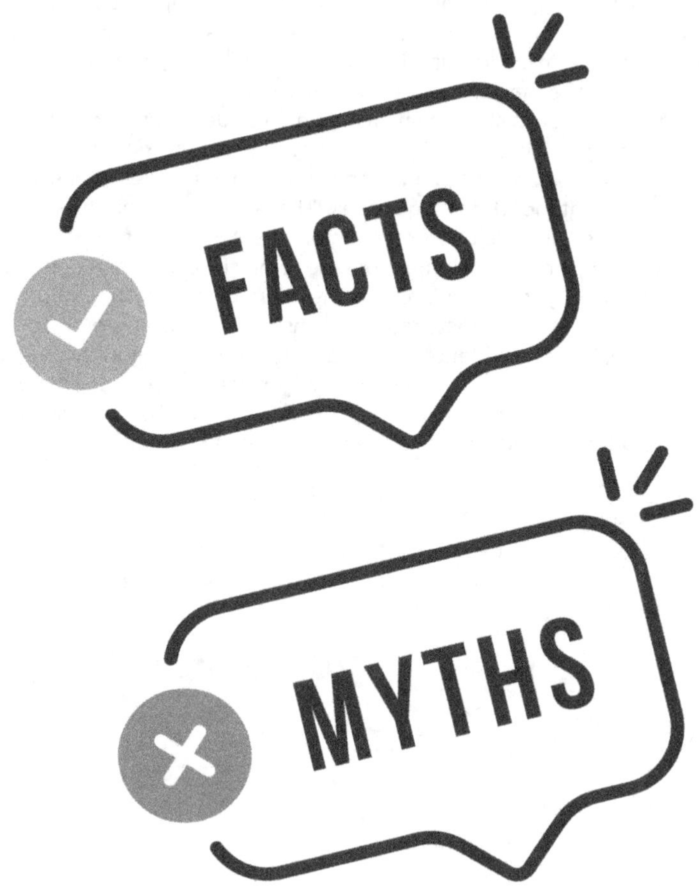

FACTS
MYTHS

Separating Fact
...from Fiction

WE'VE journeyed through the unexpected twists and turns of invention, witnessing how chance encounters and happy accidents can shape our world. Now, let's delve into a realm where fact and fiction intertwine in a captivating dance: the world of urban legends and enduring mysteries. These tales, whispered from generation to generation, often blend a kernel of truth with a generous helping of exaggeration, speculation, and pure imagination. Untangling the threads of reality from the tapestry of folklore requires a discerning eye and a healthy dose of skepticism.

Consider, for instance, the enduring legend of the Jersey Devil. This winged, horned creature, said to terrorize the Pine Barrens of New Jersey, has captured the imagination for centuries. While sightings are frequently reported—often fuelled by swamp gas, unusual bird formations, or even mischievous pranks— no conclusive evidence exists to confirm its existence. Yet, the legend persists, a testament to the power of storytelling and the human desire to believe in the extraordinary. The very ambiguity surrounding the Jersey Devil fuels its enduring appeal. Its lack of concrete proof allows each generation to reinterpret the tale, weaving their own anxieties and fears into the narrative. Is it a cryptid? A hoax? Or simply a manifestation of collective anxieties about the wilderness? The answer, perhaps, lies in the grey areas between reality and imagination.

The power of urban legends extends far beyond the realm of monstrous creatures. Think of the supposed curse of the Pharaohs, a widely believed notion that those who disturb the resting places of ancient Egyptian royalty are doomed to suffer misfortune. While several historical figures connected with the excavation of Egyptian tombs experienced untimely deaths, the reality is far more mundane: the conditions in the tombs, filled with dust, bacteria, and potentially harmful fungi, certainly posed health risks. The "curse," therefore, is more likely a case of coincidences being attributed to supernatural causes, a common phenomenon known as confirmation bias. We tend to notice instances that support our beliefs and dismiss those that contradict them.

Moving from ancient curses to modern anxieties, consider the enduring myth of the killer clowns. While certainly fuelled by genuinely disturbing events and sensationalist media coverage, the fear of clowns lurking in the shadows disproportionately amplified by the power of social media and the propagation of misinformation. Fear often thrives on the unknown, and the ambiguous nature of a clown's makeup, simultaneously playful and unnerving, can easily evoke unease, especially in vulnerable populations. This fear is further exacerbated by carefully orchestrated pranks and viral videos, which capitalize on the existing anxieties to create a narrative of impending doom. The result is a collective fear which overshadows the simple truth: the vast majority of clowns are harmless entertainers.

The prevalence of urban legends highlights the human tendency to seek patterns, even where none exist. Our brains are wired to connect disparate events and find explanations for seemingly random occurrences. This instinct, while generally beneficial for survival, can lead to the creation of elaborate narratives where simple explanations are sufficient. The power of storytelling, the human need for explanation, and the propagation of misinformation via the internet have created a fertile breeding ground for urban legends to thrive.

Another intriguing example is the enduring mystery surrounding the disappearance of Amelia Earhart. Her vanishing over the Pacific Ocean in 1937 sparked endless speculation and spawned countless theories, ranging from plane malfunctions to capture by the Japanese. While the exact circumstances remain unknown, a variety of factors contributed to the persistence of the mystery. The vastness of the Pacific, the limited technology of the time, and the ensuing World War II all hindered the search and investigation efforts, leaving ample room for speculation and conjecture. This ambiguity fuelled countless books, documentaries, and even fictional works, each adding to the enduring mystery. The ongoing search for evidence—from supposed artefacts to possible crash sites—serves as a testament to the enduring allure of unsolved mysteries.

Let's not forget the age-old tale of the Loch Ness Monster, Nessie. The murky depths of Loch Ness, coupled with occasional blurry photographs and sonar readings, have fuelled the belief in this elusive creature for nearly a century. While the chances of a plesiosaur-like creature surviving undiscovered are exceptionally slim, the legend continues to draw tourists and researchers alike. The mystique of the unknown, combined with the enduring human fascination with the extraordinary, ensures the story of Nessie will persist for generations to come.

Similarly, the mystery of the Zodiac Killer, a serial killer who terrorized Northern California in the late 1960s and early 1970s, continues to fascinate and terrify. His cryptic ciphers, taunting letters, and the unresolved nature of his identity have ensured his place in criminal folklore. The Zodiac Killer's case highlights the limitations of investigative techniques in the past, as well as the chilling impact of a seemingly unstoppable criminal. The enduring fascination stems from the unsolved nature of the case, creating a space for endless speculation and debate. Each new piece of evidence—or perceived evidence—fuels further investigation and discussion.

The persistence of urban legends and mysteries underscores the powerful role of storytelling in shaping our understanding of the world. These narratives often reflect our deepest fears, anxieties, and desires, providing a framework for interpreting the unpredictable and unexplained aspects of life. By examining these narratives critically, we can gain insights into the human psyche, the power of social influence, and the fascinating interplay between fact and fiction.

The case of spontaneous human combustion is a particularly striking example. The idea that a person could spontaneously burst into flames, leaving little trace of the body aside from ash, holds a bizarre fascination for many. While there have been accounts of such incidents, scientific explanations usually involve accidental fires, often fuelled by easily combustible materials, where circumstances obscure the cause. This highlights a key component of many urban legends—the ease with which a kernel of truth can be expanded upon through rumour and speculation, eventually leading to a wildly different version of events.

Finally, consider the supposed existence of Bigfoot (Sasquatch). Decades of reported sightings, often accompanied by blurry photographs and anecdotal accounts, have sustained the legend. The very lack of definitive proof, paradoxically, fuels the intrigue. This elusive creature has become a symbol of the wilderness, representing the unknown and the untamed aspects of nature. The enduring mystery, however, is interwoven with various theories, from elaborate hoaxes to misunderstood animal behaviour. Like other enduring legends, the story of Bigfoot plays on our desire to believe in something extraordinary, something that lies beyond the realm of the ordinary.

The study of urban legends and mysteries offers a unique lens through which to examine human behaviour, cultural values, and the ever-evolving relationship between fact and fiction. While separating truth from fiction often requires careful analysis and critical thinking, the process itself is a fascinating exploration into the human imagination and the enduring power of storytelling. Ultimately, the mysteries themselves may remain unsolved, but the questions they raise continue to enrich our understanding of the world around us and the stories we tell ourselves. The enduring appeal of these mysteries is not only in the possibility of a hidden truth but in the stories we collectively create to try and explain the inexplicable. They serve as a testament to the human desire for understanding and the power of narrative to shape our perception of reality.

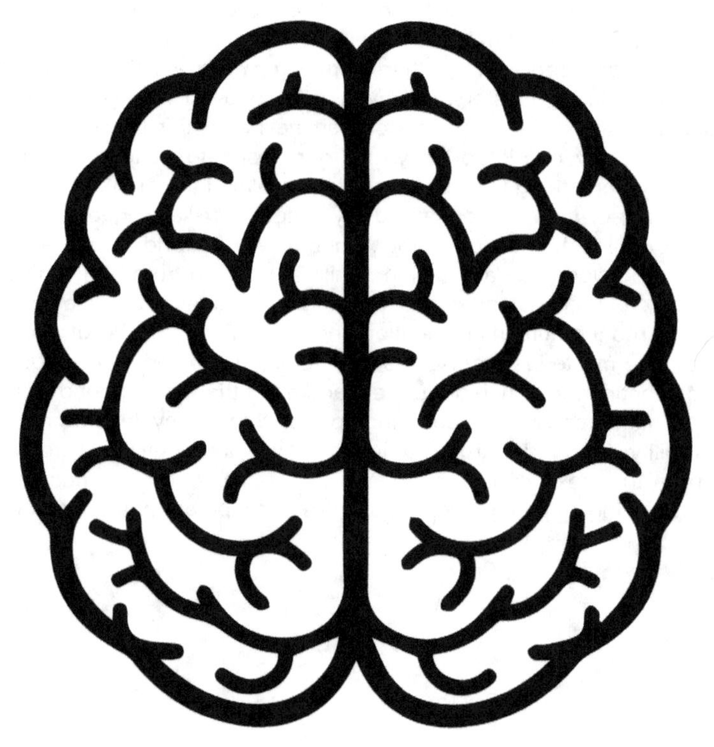

Unexpected Tricks
of the Mind

OUR journey through the unexpected continues, shifting now from the realm of urban legends and enduring mysteries to the equally baffling, and far more internal, landscape of the human mind. Forget elaborate conspiracies and shadowy figures; the most perplexing enigmas often reside within our own skulls. The human brain, a three-pound marvel of biological engineering, is capable of breathtaking feats of creativity, logic, and empathy. But it's also prone to some truly bizarre quirks, cognitive blind spots, and downright bewildering illusions. Let's explore some of the most fascinating, and sometimes frustrating, psychological phenomena that showcase the mind's unexpected tricks.

One such phenomenon is confirmation bias, a cognitive bias where we tend to favour information that confirms our pre-existing beliefs while dismissing contradictory evidence. This isn't simply stubbornness; it's a deeply ingrained mental shortcut that simplifies the overwhelming influx of information we receive daily. Think of someone who believes climate change is a hoax. They might readily accept articles and social media posts that deny climate change while actively ignoring or dismissing peer-reviewed scientific studies showing the contrary. This isn't necessarily a sign of malicious intent; it's the brain's efficient, albeit flawed, attempt to make sense of a complex world. The same principle applies to any deeply held belief, from political affiliations to dietary preferences. Understanding confirmation bias is crucial to fostering critical thinking and open-mindedness, urging us to actively seek out dissenting opinions and engage in constructive dialogue.

Then there's the Baader-Meinhof phenomenon, also known as the frequency illusion. Have you ever learned a new word, only to seemingly encounter it everywhere you look afterward? Or discovered a particular car model, only to see it suddenly on every street corner? This isn't a sudden increase in the word's or car's prevalence; it's your brain suddenly noticing something it previously overlooked. Once you've become aware of something new, your brain is more attuned to it, making it seem far more common than it actually is. This illusion highlights the selective nature of our attention and how our perceptions are heavily influenced by our prior knowledge and expectations.

The power of suggestion is another captivating area. The placebo effect, where a seemingly inert substance produces a therapeutic effect simply because the recipient believes it will, is a testament to the mind's immense influence on the body. This effect isn't limited to medicine; it extends to various aspects of our lives. The mere suggestion that something is appealing or effective can significantly influence our perception and experience of it. Think about wine tastings: the price of a wine can drastically affect how people perceive its taste, even if the wines themselves are identical. The expectation of a higher quality, influenced by the higher price, alters the sensory experience. This highlights the intricate interplay between our minds and our senses. The placebo effect demonstrates the remarkable power of belief and expectation, a force that can even override physiological processes.

Consider the bystander effect, a chilling demonstration of how the presence of others can inhibit our helping behaviour. In situations where someone needs help, the more bystanders present, the less likely any single person is to intervene. This isn't necessarily due to apathy or selfishness; it's a complex interplay of diffusion of responsibility (the assumption that someone else will help), social influence (looking to others for cues on how to react), and fear of embarrassment or social disapproval. The Kitty Genovese murder, though debated in its specifics, became a stark example of the bystander effect, highlighting the dangers of inaction in emergencies. Understanding this phenomenon is crucial in promoting prosocial behaviour and encouraging active intervention in times of need.

The framing effect, a common cognitive bias, reveals how the way information is presented can significantly impact our decisions. The same information presented in two different ways can lead to drastically different choices. For example, a surgery with a 90% survival rate sounds far more appealing than the same surgery with a 10% mortality rate, even though they describe the exact same outcome. Marketing and advertising leverage this effect extensively, shaping our choices through careful wording and presentation. Recognizing the framing effect allows us to become more critical consumers of information, less susceptible to manipulative tactics.

Optical illusions, while seemingly simple visual tricks, offer profound insights into how our brains process and interpret sensory information. From the Müller-Lyer illusion (where two lines of equal length appear different lengths) to the impossible triangle (a figure that defies three-dimensional geometry), these illusions reveal the shortcuts and assumptions our brains make in constructing our perception of reality. These shortcuts, while often efficient, can lead to misinterpretations and distorted perceptions of the world around us.

Cognitive dissonance, a state of mental discomfort arising from holding two conflicting beliefs or ideas simultaneously, often leads to intriguing mental gymnastics to resolve the inconsistency. We might change our beliefs, rationalize our actions, or simply ignore the conflicting information. For example, a smoker who knows smoking is harmful might downplay the risks or rationalize their behaviour by focusing on the pleasure derived from smoking. This demonstrates our innate desire for cognitive consistency and our remarkable ability to justify even self-contradictory actions.

The Dunning-Kruger effect, a fascinatingly ironic phenomenon, describes the tendency for unskilled individuals to overestimate their abilities while highly skilled individuals tend to underestimate theirs. This stems from the fact that a lack of skill prevents individuals from accurately assessing their own competence. The more knowledge and skill one possesses, paradoxically, the more one appreciates the breadth and depth of what they don't know. This effect highlights the importance of humility and the continuous pursuit of knowledge and self-improvement.

Finally, let's consider the power of memory, a remarkably complex and often unreliable system. Our memories are not perfect recordings of past events; they are reconstructions, subject to distortions, biases, and outright fabrication. The misinformation effect demonstrates how easily our memories can be altered by suggestive questioning or exposure to misleading information. Eyewitness testimony, often considered a cornerstone of the justice system, is surprisingly vulnerable to such distortions. The fallibility of memory underlines the importance of critical evaluation and the need for corroborating evidence when dealing with accounts of past events. The human mind, far from being a flawlessly logical machine, is a fascinating tapestry of cognitive biases, mental shortcuts, and unexpected illusions. Understanding these psychological phenomena allows us to better appreciate the complexities of human behaviour, navigate the challenges of social interaction, and make more informed decisions in all aspects of our lives. This exploration into the mind's unexpected tricks is not just intellectually stimulating; it's a journey towards self-awareness, enabling us to interpret not only the world around us, but also the intricate workings of our own internal landscapes, uncovering a world of fascinating enigmas, every bit as compelling as any urban legend or historical mystery. The seemingly simple acts of perception, decision-making, and recollection are complex processes shaped by a myriad of interacting factors, constantly reminding us of the ever-present interplay between our internal world and the external reality we perceive. The study of the human mind, in its quirks and contradictions, reveals an intricate and captivating world of surprises waiting to be discovered, a testament to the enduring capacity for wonder at the very heart of our being. And this, perhaps more than anything, underscores the fascinating and ongoing journey of understanding the human condition.

Numbers You Never Knew

HAVING delved into the surprising twists and turns of the human mind, we now shift our focus to a realm equally perplexing and profoundly beautiful: the world of mathematics. Often perceived as a rigid and unforgiving discipline, mathematics, upon closer inspection, reveals a landscape teeming with unexpected patterns, astonishing coincidences, and numbers that defy easy categorization. This is a world where seemingly random occurrences reveal underlying order, and where simple equations unlock profound truths about the universe. Prepare to be amazed by the mathematical marvels that lie hidden in plain sight, numbers that whisper secrets only the curious and observant can decipher.

Let's begin with a number that has fascinated mathematicians and mystics for millennia: π (pi). This seemingly simple ratio of a circle's circumference to its diameter, approximately 3.14159, is in reality an irrational number, meaning its decimal representation goes on forever without repeating. The pursuit of calculating π to ever greater precision has captivated mathematicians for centuries, driving advancements in computational power and revealing intricate connections between seemingly disparate areas of mathematics. While the ancient Babylonians and Egyptians had remarkably accurate approximations, the quest to pin down its true value continues to this day, a testament to its enduring allure and the boundless nature of mathematical exploration. Modern supercomputers have calculated π to trillions of digits, yet its infinite nature remains a source of both wonder and ongoing research, pushing the limits of our computational abilities and our understanding of its fundamental properties.

But π isn't the only number with an infinite decimal expansion. Consider the square root of two ($\sqrt{2}$), a number that arose naturally in geometry as the diagonal of a unit square. Its irrationality, discovered by the ancient Greeks, shattered their belief in the perfection of numbers and marked a turning point in the history of mathematics. The realization that some numbers are inexpressible as simple fractions had profound consequences, challenging fundamental assumptions about the nature of reality and ushering in a new era of mathematical sophistication. The discovery also led to further investigations into irrational and transcendental numbers, numbers that cannot be the root of any polynomial equation with integer coefficients, a field that continues to fascinate mathematicians today. The implications of these seemingly abstract mathematical concepts extend far beyond theoretical pursuits; they are fundamental to our understanding of physical phenomena and the design of many aspects of modern technology.

Another fascinating area lies in the realm of prime numbers. These numbers, divisible only by one and themselves, are the building blocks of all other integers. Their distribution among the natural numbers seems, at first glance, completely random. However, deeper investigation reveals intricate patterns and connections, prompting centuries of research and fuelling ongoing debates about the nature of prime number distribution. The Prime Number Theorem, for instance, provides an approximation of the frequency of prime numbers, but the exact distribution remains a captivating enigma, challenging mathematicians to refine existing models and formulate entirely new ones. Moreover, the quest to find ever-larger prime numbers is a continuous drive in the field, pushing the boundaries of computational power and highlighting the fundamental importance of prime numbers in cryptography and secure communication. The seemingly simple prime numbers are, in reality, complex and endlessly fascinating, holding secrets that have captivated mathematicians for centuries and continue to hold implications for contemporary technology.

Beyond the realm of single numbers, we find fascinating patterns in numerical sequences. The Fibonacci sequence, perhaps the most famous example, begins with 0 and 1, with each subsequent number being the sum of the two preceding ones (0, 1, 1, 2, 3, 5, 8, 13, and so on). This seemingly simple sequence appears surprisingly often in nature, from the arrangement of leaves on a stem to the spiral patterns in sunflowers. The ratios of consecutive Fibonacci numbers approximate the Golden Ratio (approximately 1.618), a number with its own rich history and surprising presence in art, architecture, and natural phenomena. This remarkable connection between a seemingly arbitrary mathematical sequence and the natural world underscores the profound power of mathematics to reveal underlying order in seemingly chaotic systems.

Moving into the realm of geometry, consider the remarkable properties of fractals. These intricate, self-similar patterns repeat themselves at ever-smaller scales, creating shapes of infinite complexity. From the branching of trees to the contours of coastlines, fractals are ubiquitous in nature, demonstrating the mathematical elegance underlying the complexity of the natural world. The Mandelbrot set, a particularly famous fractal, is generated by a simple iterative equation, yet the resulting image is of infinite intricacy, containing within it an endless array of miniature copies of itself. The mathematical principles underpinning fractals have found applications in diverse fields, from computer graphics to the modelling of natural processes. These seemingly abstract mathematical entities provide powerful tools for understanding complex systems, revealing patterns that would remain otherwise hidden.

Let's not forget the surprising power of mathematical paradoxes. These seemingly contradictory statements, often arising from seemingly straightforward assumptions, challenge our intuitive understanding of mathematics and reality. Zeno's paradoxes, for example, questioned the possibility of motion, using seemingly logical arguments to demonstrate that an object could never reach its destination. While these paradoxes may initially seem nonsensical, they've played a crucial role in the development of mathematical thought, prompting a deeper understanding of the limits of our reasoning and the need for rigorous mathematical frameworks. These paradoxes, far from being mere curiosities, force us to question our assumptions and refine our understanding of fundamental mathematical concepts.

Finally, the unexpected connections between seemingly disparate branches of mathematics are a constant source of amazement. Number theory, geometry, calculus, and algebra, each with its own unique language and methods, often reveal unexpected and profound relationships. The development of new mathematical fields often involves the unification of existing ones, revealing surprising and powerful symmetries that underscore the underlying interconnectedness of mathematical ideas. These unexpected connections and the unification of different mathematical branches constantly expand our understanding of the universe and our ability to model it accurately.

The world of mathematics, far from being a dry and static collection of formulas, is a dynamic and endlessly surprising landscape of patterns, paradoxes, and unexpected connections. The numbers we encounter daily, often taken for granted, conceal depths of complexity and beauty that continue to fascinate and challenge mathematicians and curious minds alike. The exploration of these mathematical marvels is not merely an intellectual pursuit; it's a journey into the heart of reality itself, revealing the intricate and elegant structure underlying the universe we inhabit. The journey into the world of numbers is a journey of continuous discovery, constantly revealing new wonders and pushing the boundaries of our understanding. So, the next time you encounter a number, consider its potential for hidden complexity, and allow your curiosity to be your guide into the intriguing world of mathematical enigmas.

Fast Facts...

Fast Facts...

Weird Science

Bananas Are Radioactive
Bananas contain potassium-40, a naturally occurring radioactive isotope. But you'd need to eat 10 million bananas in one sitting to glow. Challenge not accepted.

You're Taller in the Morning
Gravity compresses your spine throughout the day, so when you wake up, you're about 1 cm taller. The bad news? Life literally drags you down.

Octopuses Have Three Hearts
Two hearts pump blood to the gills, while the third pumps it to the body. Fun fact: when an octopus swims, the heart supplying its body *stops*. No wonder they prefer crawling.

A Day on Venus Is Longer Than Its Year
Venus rotates so slowly on its axis that one day lasts 243 Earth days, but its orbit around the sun takes only 225. Venus: where time drags and years fly.

Sharks Pre-date Trees
Sharks have existed for over 400 million years—making them older than trees, which first appeared 350 million years ago. Not just apex predators, but ancient ones too.

Water Can Boil and Freeze Simultaneously
It's called the *triple point*, and it happens when temperature and pressure are just right. Science doesn't always make sense, but it's fun to watch.

Hot Water Freezes Faster Than Cold Water
Known as the Mpemba Effect, scientists are still scratching their heads over this one. The freezer works in mysterious ways.

Humans Glow in the Dark
Humans emit a small amount of bioluminescence. It's invisible to the naked eye, but cameras sensitive enough can pick it up. You really are glowing.

There's a Planet Made of Diamonds
Planet 55 Cancri e is twice the size of Earth and composed largely of carbon. Its surface likely sparkles with diamonds. Too bad it's 40 light years away.

Honey Never Spoils
Archaeologists discovered 3,000-year-old honey in ancient Egyptian tombs—and it was still edible. Food expiration dates are shaking in their boots.

Space Smells Like Seared Steak
Astronauts have reported that space smells metallic and oddly like grilled meat. BBQ, but make it intergalactic.

Lightning Creates Glass
When lightning strikes sand, it can fuse the grains into glass structures called fulgurites. Nature's way of showing off its artistic side.

The Eiffel Tower Grows Taller in Summer
Heat causes the metal to expand, making the Eiffel Tower grow by about 6 inches during hot weather. It's France's favourite shape-shifter.

Humans Share 60% of Their DNA With Bananas
The next time someone calls you a fruitcake, they're only 40% wrong.

Cats Have Been to Space
In 1963, a French cat named Félicette was launched into space and safely returned to Earth. Space exploration? Purr-fect.

A Single Teaspoon of Honey Equals a Bee's Lifetime of Work
It takes about 12 bees working their entire lives to produce just one teaspoon of honey. Appreciate every drop.

Ants Can't Sleep
Ants take short rest periods but never truly sleep. It's no wonder they're always busy.

Cows Have Accents
Cows from different regions moo differently, depending on their herd's location. Regional accents aren't just for humans.

Goldfish Have a Longer Attention Span Than You
The myth of the 3-second goldfish memory is false. Goldfish can remember things for months. Can you say the same about where your keys are?

The Earth's Core Is as Hot as the Sun's Surface
The temperature of the Earth's core is about 5,500°C—roughly the same as the surface of the sun. Talk about a fiery heart.

Animal Antics

Penguins Propose With Pebbles
Male penguins "pop the question" by offering pebbles to females. If she accepts, it goes into the nest. Who needs jewellery when you've got stones?

Cows Have Best Friends
Cows form close social bonds, and when separated from their BFFs, they show signs of stress. Moo-d swings are real.

Wombat Poop Is Cube-Shaped
Wombats produce cube-shaped poop to stop it from rolling away and mark their territory. Proof that nature loves a straight edge.

Sloths Only Poop Once a Week
A sloth descends to the ground once a week just to relieve itself—making it nature's least enthusiastic toilet-goer.

Elephants Are Excellent Swimmers
Despite their size, elephants can swim long distances and use their trunks as snorkels. Move over, Aquaman.

Crows Can Hold Grudges
Crows remember human faces and have been known to "warn" their friends about people who annoy them. Don't cross a crow.

Koalas Have Fingerprints
Koala fingerprints are so similar to humans' that even forensic experts have been fooled. Criminal koalas remain at large.

A Group of Flamingos Is Called a 'Flamboyance'
Could there be a better name for a bunch of hot pink birds?

Pigeons Can Do Maths
Pigeons have been trained to recognize numbers and perform basic arithmetic. Turns out, they're more than just bread thieves.

Some Turtles Breathe Through Their Butts
The Fitzroy River turtle can absorb oxygen through its rear end. Nature's version of multitasking.

Human Oddities

Napoleon Was Average Height
At 5'6", Napoleon was perfectly average for his time. Blame British propaganda for turning him into the world's shortest sore loser.

You Can't Tickle Yourself
Your brain knows you're about to tickle yourself and cancels out the sensation. Self-surprise: impossible.

The Pringles Coffin
Fred Baur, inventor of the Pringles can, loved his design so much he was buried in one. Cremation: pop, don't stop.

Your Nose Can Detect 1 Trillion Smells
Your olfactory receptors can pick up a trillion distinct odours—most of which you'll never want to smell again.

The Shortest War in History Lasted 38 Minutes
The Anglo-Zanzibar War of 1896 ended in just 38 minutes. Someone was clearly in a hurry to leave.

Strange Inventions

The First Alarm Clocks Only Rang Once
Early alarm clocks could only be set for one time—and rang just once. No snooze button for the 18th century crowd!

Bubble Wrap Was Originally Wallpaper
Invented as textured wallpaper, bubble wrap never took off in home decor. Thankfully, it found its true calling in stress relief.

Toilet Paper Was Once Considered a Luxury
In 19th century America, toilet paper was so rare that it was considered a luxury item. Corn cobs and catalogues were the alternatives... ouch.

A Toaster Launched the First Pop-Up Ad
The first internet pop-up ad was for a toaster. It wasn't a hit—but unfortunately, the trend stuck.

Shoes With GPS Exist
There are shoes equipped with GPS trackers that send signals to your phone. Perfect for those of us who are directionally challenged.

Quirky Geography

There's a Town Named Dull That Partnered With Boring
Dull, Scotland, and Boring, Oregon, are official partner towns. Together, they form the ultimate snooze-worthy alliance.

Canada Has an Island Called "No Name"
Creativity ran out when naming this spot in Ontario. It's literally called "No Name Island."

There's a Desert That Gets Snow
The Sahara Desert, known for its scorching heat, occasionally gets snow in winter. Nature's way of saying, "Expect the unexpected."

Antarctica Is the World's Largest Desert
Despite all the ice, Antarctica qualifies as a desert because it receives so little precipitation. Frozen, dry, and lonely.

There's a Town Where Cats Outnumber Humans
In Aoshima, Japan, cats outnumber residents six to one. It's a purr-fectly feline utopia.

Greenland Is Icy, and Iceland Is Green
Iceland's Viking settlers gave Greenland its name to sound more appealing. Marketing was sneaky even in the 10th century.

Mount Everest Is Growing
The world's tallest mountain grows about 4 millimetres every year due to tectonic activity. Still reaching for the sky!

There's a Place Called Hell in Norway
Hell, Norway, is a real town—and yes, it freezes over in winter.

Alaska Has More Coastline Than the Rest of the U.S. Combined
Alaska's vast, jagged coastline stretches over 6,600 miles—more than all other U.S. states put together.

There's a Country With No Rivers
Saudi Arabia is the largest country in the world without a single river. Desert life comes with its challenges.

Mind-Bending History

Cleopatra Lived Closer to the Moon Landing Than the Pyramids
Cleopatra ruled Egypt about 2,100 years ago. The Great Pyramid of Giza was built 4,500 years ago—a bigger time gap than you think.

A Chicken Survived for 18 Months Without a Head
In 1945, a chicken named Mike survived for 18 months after its head was chopped off. Farmers fed it with an eyedropper. Mike became a sideshow star.

Napoleon Was Attacked by Bunnies
Napoleon Bonaparte once organized a rabbit hunt, but the rabbits turned on him and his men. Talk about an unexpected uprising.

Oxford University Is Older Than the Aztec Empire
Teaching at Oxford began around 1096. The Aztec Empire emerged in the 14th century. Europe was already deep into its textbooks.

The Eiffel Tower Was Almost Sold Twice
Conman Victor Lustig successfully posed as a government official and tried selling the Eiffel Tower—not once, but twice. Both times, he almost got away with it!

Julius Caesar Was Once Kidnapped by Pirates
While held for ransom, Julius Caesar criticized his captors for demanding too little money and promised to crucify them. He later kept his promise.

Abraham Lincoln Was a Champion Wrestler
Before becoming President, Lincoln won about 300 wrestling matches and was known for his strength. He only lost once.

Joan of Arc Was Once Put on Trial for Cross-Dressing
Among other charges, Joan of Arc was condemned for wearing men's clothing. Her legacy? Far stronger than her wardrobe critics.

The Leaning Tower of Pisa Has Leaned Since the Beginning
The tower started leaning during construction in the 12th century due to a poor foundation. Engineers have worked ever since to stop it from toppling.

George Washington Never Lived in the White House
Construction wasn't completed until after his presidency. Washington missed out on the perks of a presidential pad.

Fascinating Food Facts

Ketchup Was Once a Medicine
In the 19th century, ketchup was marketed as a cure for indigestion and diarrhoea. Heinz must be proud.

Pineapples Were a Status Symbol
In the 18th century, pineapples were so rare and expensive that people would rent them for parties to show off their wealth.

Carrots Were Originally Purple
The first carrots were purple, yellow, or white. Orange carrots didn't appear until Dutch farmers cultivated them in the 17th century.

Peanuts Aren't Nuts
Botanically, peanuts are legumes, not nuts. They belong in the same family as peas and beans.

There's an Expensive Coffee Made From Cat Poop
Kopi Luwak coffee is made using beans that have passed through the digestive tract of civet cats. It's one of the most expensive coffees in the world.

Honey Is Bee Vomit
Honey is made when bees regurgitate nectar they've collected. Delicious, but the process isn't quite as sweet.

Oranges Aren't Always Orange
In warmer climates, oranges stay green when ripe due to high chlorophyll levels.

There's Such a Thing as Blue Wine
Gïk Blue, a Spanish wine, gets its bright blue colour from pigments found in grape skin.

Apples Float in Water
Apples are made up of about 25% air, which is why they float. Perfect for apple-bobbing competitions.

Butterflies Drink Turtle Tears
Butterflies in the Amazon are known to drink the salty tears of turtles to get vital nutrients.

Amazing Space Facts

Neutron Stars Are Incredibly Dense
A sugar-cube-sized piece of a neutron star weighs about a billion tons. That's more weight than Mount Everest compressed into a cube.

Saturn Would Float in Water
Saturn's density is so low that if you could find a bathtub big enough, the gas giant would float.

A Day on Jupiter Lasts 10 Hours
Jupiter rotates so quickly that its day is only 10 hours long—the shortest in the solar system.

Venus Spins Backwards
Venus rotates in the opposite direction to most planets, meaning the sun rises in the west and sets in the east.

There's a Planet Where It Rains Glass
On HD 189733b, it rains molten glass sideways at 4,500 mph due to intense winds. Bring a sturdy umbrella.

Black Holes Aren't Black
Black holes appear black because light can't escape their gravity. They're technically invisible, but we detect them by their effects on nearby matter.

Stars Can Sneeze
Stars release powerful bursts of gas known as stellar burps, ejecting material into space. A cosmic sneeze... sort of!

Premier League Football

The Premier League Started in 1992
Formed after clubs in the old First Division broke away, the Premier League changed English football forever.

The Fastest Goal in Premier League History
Shane Long holds the record for the fastest goal, scoring just 7.69 seconds after kickoff for Southampton against Watford in 2019.

The Only Undefeated Premier League Season
Arsenal's 2003-2004 "Invincibles" went the entire season unbeaten. They remain the only team in Premier League history to achieve this feat.

Most Goals Scored in a Single Season
Erling Haaland broke records with 36 goals in the 2022-2023 season for Manchester City, surpassing previous greats.

Goalkeepers that Score Goals
Peter Schmeichel became the first Premier League goalkeeper to score a goal in 2001 for Aston Villa.

The Biggest Premier League Win
The mighty Manchester United thrashed Ipswich Town 9-0 in 1995. Leicester City and Liverpool later equalled this record.

The Longest Premier League Match
The match between Arsenal and West Ham in 2019 lasted an epic 102 minutes, including added time.

Premier League Is Broadcast in Over 200 Countries
The league reaches an estimated 3.2 billion people worldwide each season. Football truly is the global game.

Manchester City Won the League With 100 Points
In the 2017-2018 season, Manchester City earned 100 points—the most in Premier League history.

Only One Team Has Scored 100 Goals in a Season Twice
Manchester City achieved this remarkable feat in the 2017-18 and 2019-20 campaigns.

The World of Wine

The Oldest Bottle of Wine Is Over 1,600 Years Old
The Speyer wine bottle, found in a Roman tomb in Germany, dates back to 325 AD. Nobody wants to taste-test it, and probably not the best drop to accompany a cheese board.

Red Wine Gets Its Colour From Grape Skins
The juice of most grapes is clear. Red wine's colour comes from the grape skins during fermentation.

The World's Most Expensive Bottle of Wine
A bottle of 1945 Romanée-Conti sold for $558,000 at auction in 2018. That's one pricey sip.

Champagne Can Only Come From Champagne
Sparkling wines made anywhere else can't be legally called "champagne."

The Term 'Vintage' Refers to the Year
In wine, "vintage" refers to the year the grapes were harvested,
not how old the bottle is.

Wine Was Once Prescribed as Medicine
In the Middle Ages, doctors prescribed wine to cure illnesses ranging from digestive problems to depression. Best crack open the Chardonnay.

The World's Oldest Wine Region
Georgia (the country, not the U.S. state) is home to the oldest evidence of wine making, dating back over 8,000 years.

Wines Age Differently Based on Storage
Storing wine on its side prevents the cork from drying out, which helps the wine age properly.

Not All Wines Improve With Age
Most wines are made to be enjoyed young. Only a small percentage are meant for long-term aging.

The Largest Wine Cellar Holds 2 Million Bottles
The Milestii Mici cellar in Moldova holds over 2 million bottles of wine and spans 120 miles underground.

Fun Physics

Gravity Is Stronger at the Poles
Earth's gravity is slightly stronger at the poles than at the equator because the planet bulges at the equator.

Light Can Bend Around Objects
Light can bend when it passes through gravitational fields—a phenomenon called gravitational lensing.

You're Moving Even When Standing Still
Earth rotates at about 1,000 miles per hour at the equator. You're always on the move, whether you know it or not. Flat Earther's take note!!

Time Slows Down at High Speeds
According to Einstein's theory of relativity, time slows down the faster you travel.

Sound Travels Faster Through Solids
Sound waves move faster through solids than liquids or gases because the particles are closer together.

The Speed of Light Is the Cosmic Speed Limit
Nothing in the universe can travel faster than the speed of light—186,282 miles per second.

Water Can Flow Uphill in a Narrow Tube
Capillary action allows water to flow upward in narrow spaces, defying gravity.

An Object in Motion Stays in Motion
Newton's first law of motion states that an object will remain in motion unless acted upon by an external force.